Reason To Write

Strategies for Success in Academic Writing

ADVANCED

Mary R. Colonna
and
Judith E. Gilbert

Series Editors
Robert F. Cohen and Judy L. Miller

OXFORD
UNIVERSITY PRESS

OXFORD
UNIVERSITY PRESS

198 Madison Avenue
New York, NY 10016 USA

Great Clarendon Street, Oxford OX2 6DP UK

Oxford University Press is a department of the University of Oxford.
It furthers the University's objective of excellence in research,
scholarship, and education by publishing worldwide in

Oxford New York

Auckland Cape Town Dar es Salaam Hong Kong Karachi
Kuala Lumpur Madrid Melbourne Mexico City Nairobi
New Delhi Shanghai Taipei Toronto

With offices in

Argentina Austria Brazil Chile Czech Republic France Greece
Guatemala Hungary Italy Japan Poland Portugal Singapore
South Korea Switzerland Thailand Turkey Ukraine Vietnam

OXFORD and OXFORD ENGLISH are registered trademarks of
Oxford University Press

© Oxford University Press 2006

Database right Oxford University Press (maker)

Executive Publisher: Janet Aitchison
Senior Acquisitions Editor: Pietro Alongi
Editor: Dena Daniel
Associate Editor: Scott Allan Wallick
Art Director: Maj-Britt Hagsted
Senior Designer: Michael Steinhofer
Art Editor: Judi DeSouter
Production Manager: Shanta Persaud
Production Controller: Eve Wong

ISBN-13: 978 0 19 436583 3
ISBN-10: 0 19 436583 2

Printed in the United States.

Printing (last digit): 10 9 8 7 6 5 4 3 2 1

ACKNOWLEDGEMENTS

Illustrations: Brad Walker, 1; Steven Appleby, 12; Karen Minot, 8, 19,
89, 112–113; Zina Saunders, 163

*The publishers would like to thank the following for their permission to
reproduce photographs:*

Corbis/Najlah Feanny-Hidis, 2; Randy Faris, 21; Cheryl Ravelo/
Reuters, 45; Corbis Royalty Free, 45; Greg Smith, 47; Gustave Dore,
90; Gary Salter/ZEFA, 111; Archivo Iconografico SA, 170; Bettman,
171, 172; Alamy/Juniors Bildarchiv, 4; Banana Stock, 45; Alan King,
140; The Image Works/Rhoda Sidney, 50; The Everett Collection, 91;
Masterfile/Royalty Free Division, 68; Brian Peters, 135; Guy Grenier,
142; Rick Gomez, 164

The publishers would like to thank the following for their help:

"Human Cloning Debate: Why do it? Who'd be hurt? Should it be
legal?" by Peter Kendall. Copyright © 2/23/1997 by Chicago Tribune
Company. All rights reserved. Used with permission.

"Cherries for My Grandma" by Geoffrey Canada. Copyright © 1998 by
New York Times Co. Reprinted and adapted with permission.

"Some Reflections on the Technology of Eating" by Bryce Nelson.
Copyright © 1983 by The New York Times Co. Reprinted and adapted
with permission.

Toffler's Waves by Michael Finley. Copyright © 2005 by Michael Finley.
Reprinted and adapted with permission.

"You've Got Inappropriate Mail" by Lisa Guernsey. Copyright © 2000
by New York Times Co. Reprinted and adapted with permission.

"Technology, Workplace Privacy and Personhood" from *Journal of
Business Ethics*, Volume 15, Number 11, November 1996, pp. 1237–
1248(12). Copyright © 1996 Springer. Reprinted by permission.

"The Face of Beauty" from *A Natural History of the Senses* by Diane
Ackerman. Copyright © 1990 by Diane Ackerman. Used by
permission of Vintage Books, a division of Random House, Inc.

"How You See Yourself: Potential for Big Problems" by Sandra
Blakeslee. Copyright © 1991 by The New York Times Co. Reprinted
and adapted with permission.

"My Grandfather" from *A Summer Life* by Gary Soto. Copyright © 1990
by University Press of New England. Used by permission of Bantam
Doubleday Dell Books for Young Readers, a division of Bantam
Doubleday Dell Publishing Group, Inc.

"William Sheldon's Body and Temperament Types" from *Tracking the
Elusive Human*, Volume 1, by James and Tyra Arraj. Copyright © 2005
by James and Tyra Arraj. Reprinted and adapted with permission.

Excerpt from *The Kite Runner* by Khaled Hosseini. Copyright © 2003
by Khaled Hosseini. Used in the United States by permission of
Riverhead Books, an imprint of Penguin Group (USA) Inc. Used in the
UK and Commonwealth by permission of Bloomsbury Publishing.
Used in Canada by permission of Doubleday Canada.

"Students Shall Not Download. Yeah, Sure." by Kate Zernike.
Copyright © 2003 by The New York Times Co. Reprinted and adapted
with permission.

Lecture on philosophers at Columbia University, 2004, reproduced
with permission of Dr. Joseph Chuman, Leader, Ethical Culture
Society of Bergen County, New Jersey.

AUTHOR ACKNOWLEDGEMENTS

We are grateful to Janet Aitchison and Pietro Alongi of Oxford University press for inviting us to do this project and to our editors, Dena Daniel, Robert Cohen, and Judy Miller for their encouragement and help in shaping the book.

Our thanks also go to our friends, colleagues, and students at the American Language Program at Columbia University for their comments and suggestions. In particular, we would like to thank our mentors at the ALP, Mary Jerome, Gail Fingado, Linda Lane, and Karen Brockmann. We are also grateful to John Beaumont for his help in navigating the book-writing process, to Patrick Aquilina for the "Vicious Circle," an examination of discrimination, and to Shelley Saltzman for SAFER. We would also like to thank our students: Dani Vos for his essay on umbrellas and personality, Mee Young Kim for her description of her aunt, and Juri Ogawa for her contributions to our collection of euphemisms.

We would like to acknowledge the contributions of the following people: Dr. Joseph Chuman, professor of human rights at Columbia University and Leader of the Ethical Culture Society of Bergen County for his encapsulation of the theories of three great ethicists, and Dr. Richard L. Gilbert for the handouts on theories of personality and the work of Lawrence Kohlberg.

To my husband, Spyros Harisiadis, who gave me the courage to pursue my dreams; my daughter, Soula Harisiadis, who gave me the support to achieve those dreams; and in loving memory of my nephew, Gregory Colonna, who had so little time to dream.

Mary Colonna

To Masayuki Anno and Jason Masanobu Gilbert Anno, the men in my life, for their love and support.

Judy Gilbert

REASON TO WRITE

STRATEGIES FOR SUCCESS IN ACADEMIC WRITING

Introduction

Writing teachers have a dual challenge: Not only must they help the most reticent and timid writers overcome a potentially crippling writing phobia, but they must also instill in their students the confidence needed to translate their thoughts into correct and acceptable English. The communicative approach that we use in the *Reason to Write* series will help teachers to achieve this end.

Even though the writing product is an expression of one's individuality and personality, it is important to remember that writing is also a social endeavor, a way of communicating with others, informing them, persuading them, and debating with them. In our attempt to provide guidelines, strategies, and practice in writing for university, community college, and high school students preparing for the academic demands of all disciplines in higher education, we want students to realize that they are not writing in a vacuum. They have a voice, and what they write will elicit a reaction from others. In our books writing is, therefore, an active communicative/social process involving discussion, interaction with teachers, group work, pair work, and peer evaluation. Through these collaborative experiences, students come to recognize their unique strengths while they cultivate their critical-thinking skills and become more effective writers.

Content-based themes that speak to both the hearts and minds of students are the key to realizing our goal. Writing can develop only where there is meaning; it cannot be an empty exercise in form. And meaning cannot be understood unless students are given intellectually challenging and emotionally appealing material that generates their enthusiasm. Because all instruction in grammar, vocabulary, and rhetorical styles is presented in relation to a theme, each unit provides a seamless path from reading to thinking to writing, from the preparatory stages of writing to the completion of a final written composition. Working with one theme, the whole class experiences the same problem or issue at the same time, and students benefit from the security of the shared discussion and exploration. As a result, writers are not left to suffer alone with the blank page. At the same time, students are given several writing options within each theme so that there is ample opportunity for individual expression.

Content-based themes also encourage the kind of critical thinking that students are expected to do across the curriculum in a college or university. Because many English-language learners may lack some of the analytical skills needed to do academic work, we provide them with experience in analyzing ideas, making inferences, supporting opinions, understanding points of view, and writing for different audiences. As students "reason to write," they practice the skills and strategies that are vital for academic success, and they have an opportunity to write on a wide variety of themes that reflect the academic curriculum.

The Advanced Book

This book is intended for students who will soon be expected to respond to the demands not only of the college composition course but also of the college curriculum itself. Although the students at this level need to work at becoming more comfortable with the rhetorical styles that they were first exposed to in *Reason to Write, Intermediate*, they also need to be taken a step further and be taught to summarize, synthesize, and respond. This book is therefore unique in its emphasis on summary, synthesis, and response and on the integration of these skills into a comprehensive writing experience. It also focuses on the documentation methods necessary for research papers in college courses.

Even though students negotiate more sophisticated tasks at this level, they still receive the same step-by-step guidance and support through the writing process as in the other books of the series in the five main sections of each unit.

I. Fluency Practice: Freewriting

All units begin with an unstructured writing task in which students can freely express their thoughts and share them with a partner, without worrying about grammar or spelling. In this section, students explore the theme of the unit by drawing on their own knowledge and ideas. As a result, they enter the subsequent discussions with more self-assurance.

II. Reading for Writing

In order to develop as a writer, one must be a reader. Therefore, each unit contains a provocative reading passage followed by a series of writing activities that culminate in the main writing task of the unit. In this section, students consider the meaning of the readings and also work with the vocabulary and syntactic forms needed for discussing and writing.

III. Prewriting Focus

This section prepares the students for the writing task by developing their interpretive skills. They must "read between the lines," infer the motives of the individuals in various scenarios, and write from different points of view. They are also asked to write short opinions of their own and to practice writing summaries of the opinions expressed in their group discussions. As they complete these small writing tasks, students give and receive immediate feedback through ongoing dialogue with a partner or group, building confidence for the main writing task in the next section.

IV. Structured Writing Focus

When students reach the main writing task, they realize that all their work in previous sections has prepared them for the central writing assignment. Because we feel that students should be given choices, we have provided an alternative writing task.

In this section of the unit, students are guided through a series of steps that will lead to the successful completion of the writing task. In unit one, students learn to write a summary and a response. In unit two, they review the elements of a five-paragraph essay. In subsequent units, they learn to use a summary as the point of departure for an essay, integrate quotes into paragraphs, compare research studies, and synthesize material from various sources. Throughout this journey, students practice writing introductions and conclusions, thesis statements, topic sentences, transitional sentences, and supporting details as they complete a variety of descriptive, classification, satirical, advantages and disadvantages, cause and effect, comparison and contrast, literary analysis, and argumentative essays.

To give students the support they need to accomplish the writing tasks, we provide a model for them to follow. The model is on a topic that is similar to the writing topic. Students then work through the brainstorming process and do exercises that help them prepare a first draft. After writing their first draft, they read it to a partner or a small group of students. In this way, peer evaluation becomes a regular part of the writing process and the class becomes a "writing workshop" in which the writing process is demystified and students learn how to look critically at their own work. Our guidelines for peer work ensure that this is a positive experience, a prelude but not a substitute for feedback from the teacher.

After writing a second draft, students are ready to proofread their work. At this point, the unit focuses on various editing exercises dealing with grammar and stylistics issues that present difficulties for students at this level. After completing these exercises and editing their second draft, students are ready to write the final draft.

V. Additional Writing Opportunities

We believe that students can perfect their writing skills only by writing a great deal. Therefore, in this section, we give them the opportunity to write on a wide variety of additional stimulating topics. However, this time they are writing without our step-by-step guidance. As students learn to avail themselves of this additional writing practice in each unit, they will eventually develop the skills and confidence they need to become more independent writers.

In conclusion, the *Reason to Write* series represents our effort to integrate the insights of whole language learning and writing workshops across the curriculum at the college level. These books were also written with the knowledge that no textbook can come to life and be effective without the creative contributions of the teachers and students who use it. We hope that you and your students will develop a strong connection with the material in this book and thus form a bond with us as you explore the writing process. We would appreciate any suggestions or comments you may have. You can write to us in care of Oxford University Press, AmELT, 198 Madison Avenue, New York, New York 10016.

Robert F. Cohen and Judy L. Miller

CONTENTS

Editing focus:
  clauses for comparison, contrast, and concession
  transitional expressions between sentences

1 PANDORA'S BOX

WRITING A SUMMARY AND RESPONSE

In this unit you will practice:
- identifying arguments
- summarizing
- forming and expressing a point of view

Editing focus:
- paraphrasing
- subject-verb agreement

 ## I Fluency Practice: Freewriting

Think about the title of this unit, "Pandora's Box." In an ancient Greek myth, a woman named Pandora was given a box to guard and told not to look inside. But she was too curious, and she opened the box. As a result, chaos was released into the world.

Now look at the picture above. How might cloning be like Pandora's box? What problems could result from making exact copies of people? What are some possible benefits? Is it possible to stop experimentation with cloning, or are humans too curious to leave the box closed?

Write for ten minutes. Try to express yourself as well as you can. Don't worry about mistakes. Share your writing with a partner.

II ▸ Reading for Writing

A Scottish scientist succeeded in cloning a sheep that he named Dolly. This led to great controversy and worldwide debate about cloning. Peter Kendall, a science writer for *The Chicago Tribune*, explores some of the issues involving cloning, especially human cloning.

HUMAN CLONING DEBATE: WHY DO IT? WHO'D BE HURT? SHOULD IT BE LEGAL?

Distraught because he believes he will never produce a child, a sterile man listens to a doctor explaining how he can, indeed, father a biological son. The boy would be the image of his old man,
5 the doctor says. In fact, the son would be a genetic carbon copy of his father—a clone. With all its ethical difficulties, that scenario is just one of many that leaped from fantasy to possibility with the cloning of a Scottish sheep.
10 In the past, reports of cloning experiments could be tempered by assurances that they have no applications to human beings. Not so with the experiment reported in an upcoming issue of the science journal "Nature." Cloning a mammal from
15 mature body tissue is a quantum leap toward what many have pondered and some have feared— cloning people. "This is as close to a Xerox machine as we are going to get in reproductive technology," said Glenn McGee, a bioethicist at the University of
20 Pennsylvania.
For years, ethicists have mulled over the moral values of cloning. Why would someone want to do it? Who would be hurt? Should it be legal? Now, with the cloning of "Dolly," their ruminations have new
25 importance.
In 1994, the National Advisory Board on Ethics in Reproduction (NABER) issued a report on the ethics of cloning. "NABER members find the scenario of giving birth to one's identical twin (or giving birth to
30 one's husband's identical twin) bizarre," the report said. "They maintain that to create a child with one's exact genetic constitution is narcissistic and ethically impoverished."

distraught: extremely sad

sterile: not able to reproduce

carbon copy: exact copy

tempered: softened

quantum leap: sudden advancement

pondered: thought about

ethicist: specialist in deciding what is morally right or wrong

mulled over: thought about carefully

ruminations: deep thoughts

narcissistic: self-centered

ethically impoverished: morally wrong

But is every case so <u>cut and dried</u>? The advisory
35 board's paper raised this case: What if a couple
wanted to have a child, but one partner will pass
on a <u>debilitating</u> genetic condition and neither
considers it acceptable to use <u>donor</u> eggs or sperm?
The paper concluded that these kinds of situations
40 would be so rare that they do "not justify a <u>blanket
acceptance</u> of this practice."

Many of the ethical issues raised by cloning
already are being confronted by people concerned
about the existing potential for genetic engineering
45 in human reproduction. Soon, some predict, parents
will be able to choose many of their baby's traits—
short or tall, cautious or risk-taking. "We are going
from a period of time where people had babies to
where people make babies," said McGee, author of
50 the new book, "The Perfect Baby."

The issues have resisted being sorted into <u>piles</u> of
right and wrong. "People have already had children
because they had one child who needed a <u>bone
marrow transplant</u> and needed a donor," he said.
55 "This would just be a case where, when you were
going to do that, you would be sure to have a match.
I don't think it is necessarily immoral," he said.

But humanity might not be ready for <u>asexual</u>
reproduction, with its enormous cultural implications.
60 "That we might be the same from parent to child
to grandchild is such a <u>radical departure from</u> the
normal state of things that it would require a whole
rethinking of the way we raise the next generation,"
said Gladys White, executive director of NABER.
65 Just proving that cloning humans is possible
is almost unthinkable because the very first
experiments would be <u>repugnant</u>. "To even justify
doing the experiment, you would have to say, 'What
will we do if we produce a <u>malformed</u> baby?'" said
70 Arthur Caplan, director of the Center for Bioethics at
the University of Pennsylvania. "What is the ethical
purpose of even trying?"

cut and dried: simple

debilitating: weakening
donor: given by
someone else

blanket acceptance:
acceptance of
something in all forms

piles: groups

bone marrow transplant:
replacement of diseased
tissue inside the bones

asexual: without sex

radical departure from:
extreme change from

repugnant: causing a
strong feeling of dislike

malformed: incorrectly
formed or shaped

Many of the more frightening <u>scenarios</u> that the Scottish experiment might inspire belong to science
75 fiction, however. The sheep cells used in the cloning were <u>robust</u>, living cells, not dead ones. There is no indication that, say, Abraham Lincoln's dried blood and skull fragments (on display at the National Museum of Health and Medicine in Washington,
80 D.C.) could be used to create a new Abraham Lincoln. Besides, people are much more than their genes. "If I try to create Abraham Lincoln without having him born in 1809 and having him be the president during the Civil War, he would not turn out
85 to be Abraham Lincoln," Caplan said.

scenarios: imagined situations

robust: healthy and strong

The experiments also do not imply that <u>extinct species</u>, like the long-gone <u>tyrannosaurus rex</u>, could
90 be recreated, as in [the novel] *Jurassic Park*. But what about species <u>on the verge of</u> extinction? The last passenger pigeon died
95 in a cage in a Cincinnati zoo in 1914. If in 2014, another bird is perched alone on the edge of extinction, would it be a good idea to clone it, again and again, maintaining a permanent, captive <u>flock</u> of identical, non-reproducing birds?

extinct species: animals that no longer exist

tyrannosaurus rex: a predatory dinosaur

on the verge of: very near

flock: group (birds)

100 The Scottish researchers were trying to do something much less <u>grandiose</u>. They were concerned with the same thing Scottish breeders have been working on for centuries—making <u>livestock</u> more efficient.

grandiose: on a large scale

livestock: farm animals

105 "What counts in terms of similarity in identity in a sheep is not what we value in terms of similarity of identity in people," Caplan said. "Having identical brain structures doesn't make you the same person. Having identical lamb chops, or a <u>duplicate</u> leg of mutton, is
110 interesting, though, if your goal is to eat it."

duplicate: copy

A. General Understanding

1. Identifying Arguments

List at least three benefits of cloning and three fears that people associate with cloning according to the reading. Try to put the arguments in your own words. It's not necessary to use complete sentences. With a partner, use your answers to take turns summarizing the main points of the article. Then write your own opinions about cloning in your notebook.

BENEFITS OF CLONING

1. _____

2. _____

3. _____

FEARS ABOUT CLONING

1. _____

2. _____

3. _____

2. Making Inferences

Answer these questions in your notebook. The answers may not be directly stated in the article. Use information from the article to support your inferences. Share your answers with your classmates.

1. Why do the debates over cloning now have new importance?

2. Why does choosing the traits of a child scare some people?

3. Why do most people's fears of cloning belong to science fiction?

4. Although the author presents many arguments both for and against cloning, his own personal opinion is clear to the careful reader. Does the author favor cloning or not? Explain your answer.

B. Working with Language

1. Word Search

Find the words and phrases within the text of the newspaper article on pages 2–4 that match the definitions below. Then write the words next to the definitions.

Search in lines 1–33

a. not able to have children: sterile

b. concerned with right and wrong: _____

c. loving oneself too much: _____

Search in lines 34–64

d. to give sufficient reasons for: _____

e. characteristics: _____

f. without a sense of right or wrong: _____

g. consequences: _____

Search in lines 65–110

h. no longer existing: _____

i. a class of living organisms: _____

j. the unique personality of an individual: _____

2. Word Forms

Fill in the chart with the missing forms of the words. Use a dictionary.

	Noun	Verb	Adjective	Adverb
a.	1. ethicist 2.	——		
b.		——	extinct	——
c.		——	immoral	
d.		justify		——
e.	1. 2.	——	narcissistic	——
f.			sterile	——
g.	1. clone 2.			——

3. Reproductive and Therapeutic Cloning

Complete the paragraph below using the words and expressions in the box. When you have finished, compare your answers with a partner's.

cloning	implications
cut and dried	justifies
ethically	narcissism
extinction	repugnant
immoral	species

Many people consider _____ (1) a child morally _____ (2). Wanting to create an exact duplicate of yourself is an example of _____ (3) to them. On the other hand, many of the same people argue that it is _____ (4) acceptable to use cloning to find cures for diseases. This kind of therapeutic cloning involves stem cell research, a controversial field in which scientists use cells from embryos to produce donor cells for patients. Supporters of therapeutic cloning believe that the need to cure diseases _____ (5) the use of stem cell research and therapeutic cloning.

Some religious leaders disagree. They and many other opponents of stem cell research maintain that cloning for any reason is _____ (6). For them, there is no debate; the issue is _____ (7). The future _____ (8) of therapeutic cloning frighten them. They argue that the cloning of animals to prevent the complete _____ (9) of a _____ (10) is quite different from cloning humans, whether for reproductive or therapeutic reasons.

III Prewriting Activities

A. Collecting Support for Arguments

A "roving reporter" for a newspaper asked people on the street this question: "How do you feel about the possibility of cloning?" Read the responses the reporter received. Then, in your notebook write the arguments in favor of cloning in one column and the arguments against cloning in another. Which opinions seem to favor both sides?

"Cloning people and animals are both things that people shouldn't be doing. Creation is something that God and nature alone should do. People get sick for a reason. Does anyone really want to live forever?" — *Elizabeth Lapp, 52, nurse, Seattle, WA*

"We wouldn't regret doing it. If we cloned a person, it would answer many questions, like whether or not the cloned people would have different thoughts and personalities. I'd be very interested to see what would happen." — *Dr. Hussein Al Awawdeh, 34, pediatrician, Los Angeles, CA*

"It doesn't bother me either way. It happens all the time in movies. If it's good enough for the movies, then it's good enough for me." — *Ryan Moser, 42, correctional officer, Fort Myers, FL*

"I think scientists can really improve our lives if they make clones of certain things, like organs. But who is going check that these scientists aren't secretly making some clone army?" — *Amy Tieman, 28, city planner, Boston, MA*

"Who would decide who gets cloned? I think it's just too much power for any group of people to have. All kinds of things could go wrong, I guess. But everyone would love a clone of my dog, Oscar. He's so cute." — *Vicky Cho, 34, interior designer, New York, NY*

"There are enough people in the world now. Scientists should only use this technology to cure diseases." — *Randy Nelson, 24, law student, Albuquerque, NM*

"If a scientist clones a person and then that person dies because of a DNA mistake the scientist made, does that mean the scientist killed that person? Perhaps we should wait until we can be sure of what we're doing." — *Anthony Zak, 48, teacher, Detroit, MI*

"Cloning humans could solve so many problems it will only be a matter of time before a scientist somewhere does it. It's a much better idea if it's done sooner in a safe way instead of later by some crazy scientist." — *Laurel Barnes, 54, librarian, San Antonio, TX*

"It will be great for saving the environment. No more animals will become extinct. And the more we learn about cloning, the more we can improve what nature has given us." — *Yumi Nakayama, 21, student, Chicago, IL*

Now discuss your answers in a small group. Which opinions were also mentioned in the article? Which opinions do you agree or disagree with?

B. Using Your Own Words to Respond to Arguments

Express how you feel about cloning by responding to the arguments you have read so far. In your notebooks, respond to at least three of the arguments by completing this sentence. Be sure to put the arguments in your own words, as simply as possible.

I can/can't understand why _____ feels that _____

because _____.

Example:

I can understand why Vicky Cho feels that it would be a great idea to clone her dog because I would love to clone my cat.

C. Open for Discussion

Discuss these questions in a small group. Then choose one question and summarize the group's discussion in writing in your notebook.

1. If cloning becomes a reality, how will it affect the future of society? For example, what role will men have in society if they are no longer needed to reproduce?

2. Is it acceptable to clone human stem cells to save lives or cure diseases?

3. Would it be acceptable to clone humans for body parts?

4. How do you feel about genetically engineered babies? Do parents have the right to create the "perfect baby"? What traits would you choose for your child? What problems could this create for society?

5. What are the advantages and disadvantages of genetically engineered plants?

6. A cat was recently cloned for $50,000. Would you clone a favorite pet? Why or why not? How much would you be willing to pay to clone a pet?

IV **Structured Writing Focus**

 YOUR TASK

Write a summary of and a response to the article "Human Cloning Debate: Why Do It? Who Would Be Hurt? Should It Be Legal?"

ALTERNATIVE TASK: **Choose another article from a newspaper, magazine, or the Internet on the subject of genetic engineering: human cloning, animal cloning, stem cell research, or genetic engineering of plants. Write a summary and response in two or three paragraphs.**

A. Starting to Write

1. Brainstorming

Thinking about a topic before beginning a writing assignment helps the writer formulate arguments and gather support for them. There are many different ways to **brainstorm**.

Read the list of brainstorming techniques. Discuss them with a partner to make sure you understand them. Then discuss which ones work best for you.

TECHNIQUES FOR BRAINSTORMING

- Write down any ideas on a topic, in no particular order.
- Talk ideas over with a classmate and take notes.
- Make a flow chart of main points.
- Write an outline of ideas.
- Use a combination of these techniques.

2. Questions to Get You Started

Look back at your answers in General Understanding on page 5 and the Prewriting Activities on pages 8–9 to start brainstorming for your essay. Consider these questions and take notes in your notebook for the writing task you've chosen.

FOR THE MAIN AND ALTERNATIVE TASKS

What is the main idea of this article?
What arguments does the author use to support his opinions?
Are the author's arguments convincing?
Do you agree or disagree with the author's opinions?
What other factors should be considered when discussing this subject?

10   Unit 1

B. Preparing the First Draft

1. Writing a Summary

A **summary** is generally a shortened version of the material. The summary must be expressed in your own words. You can write a summary about a discussion, a piece of writing, or even a cartoon. Your summary should only include the most important information; it should *not* include your personal opinion.

When thinking about a summary, ask yourself these questions:
What is this about?
What is the author trying to say about this topic?

When writing your summary, follow these steps:

- Begin with a **topic sentence** that expresses the main focus of the summary.

  A topic sentence includes the topic, what is being said about the topic, and where your information is from.

- Write the **body** of the paragraph to support the main focus.

  Decide how the article is organized. For example, it might be organized into advantages and disadvantages. Then write the most important information from each category.

- Write a **concluding sentence** that restates the main focus.

Study this block diagram of a summary to help you organize your summary. In your notebook, draw your own diagram and write notes in each of its sections.

TOPIC SENTENCE
Topic
What is being said about the topic
Where your information is from

BODY OF PARAGRAPH
Support for topic
Paraphrased information

CONCLUDING SENTENCE
Restatement of topic sentence

Read the cartoon and the summary of it.

CLONES ~ THE FUTURE! | Steven Appleby

A BASKETBALL TEAM.

Unfortunately we all play the same position.

A BOSS AND HIS 'YES' MEN.

Am I right?

YES!

The New York Times February 26, 1997

Summary

In this cartoon from <u>The New York Times</u> newspaper, the artist is trying to show in a comical way the advantages and disadvantages of cloning. On the left, he draws a picture of a basketball team whose players all look the same. The reader's first response is to think of the possibilities of a team full of fabulous players like Michael Jordan. The humor in the cartoon comes from the fact that the players can only play one position, which would certainly be a disadvantage to a team. On the right, the artist shows us a similar situation in the business world. A group of employees are all agreeing with the boss. Some people feel this is an ideal situation for a boss, so being able to clone your employees seems like an advantage. In this cartoon, the artist shows us both positive and negative possibilities for cloning.

2. Analyzing a Summary Paragraph

Answer these questions to analyze the organization of the summary above.

1. Where is the topic sentence? Label it. What information does it contain?

_____

_____

2. Which sentence repeats the same idea as the first sentence? What is it called? Label it.

_____

_____

3. What is the job of the other sentences in the paragraph? Label them.

_____

_____

3. Writing a Response

Unlike a summary, a **response** should clearly give your opinion on the topic under discussion.

When thinking about a response, ask yourself these questions:
How do I feel about this topic?
How can I support my opinions?

> **When writing your response, follow these steps:**
> - Begin with a **topic sentence** that states what you are responding to and how you feel about it.
> - Write the **body** of the paragraph to support your point of view. This can come from the original source or from your own experience.
> - Write a **concluding sentence** that restates your opinion on the topic.

Study this block diagram of a response to help you organize your response. In your notebook, draw your own diagram and write notes in each of its sections.

TOPIC SENTENCE
What you are responding to
How you feel about it

BODY OF PARAGRAPH
Support for your opinion
Examples

CONCLUDING SENTENCE
Restatement of your opinion

Read the model response based on the cartoon on page 12.

> **Response**
>
> This cartoon clearly demonstrates that cloning can be harmful to society. I, too, would love to be able to clone certain people, such as Michael Jordan or Albert Einstein. Unfortunately, as you see in the first cartoon, when scientists interfere with nature they usually create new problems. The second cartoon at first might seem positive, but it also shows us some problems with cloning. If employees always think exactly like their boss, there will be fewer new ideas in a company. This can hurt a company a lot. These cartoons show that the effects of cloning on our future society can be harmful.

4. Analyzing a Response Paragraph

Answer these questions to analyze the response above.

1. In which sentence does the writer first give his opinion of cloning? What is his opinion?

   _____

   _____

2. What support does he give for his opinion? Is his support based on the cartoon or his own experience?

   _____

   _____

3. Which key word is repeated in the concluding sentence?

   _____

   _____

*Write a **first draft** of your summary and response. Remember to write in complete sentences and try to use some of the vocabulary and structures that you have practiced in this unit.*

C. Revising the First Draft

When you have finished writing your first draft, read it to a partner.

CHECKLIST FOR REVISING THE FIRST DRAFT

When you listen to your partner's essay and when you discuss your own, keep these questions in mind:

1. Does the topic sentence of your summary identify the piece being summarized?

2. Does your summary organize the main points into categories?

3. Whose opinions are stated in the summary?

4. Does the topic sentence of your response state your opinion?

5. Do you use your own words as much as possible? If you used someone else's words, did you use quotation marks and indicate who said them?

6. Did you support your opinions? Is your support from the story or from another source?

7. Does your conclusion refer back to the beginning of the paragraph or essay?

After discussing your essay with your partner, you may want to add new ideas, include more support, and/or adjust your conclusion.

*Now write a **second draft** that includes all of your additions and changes.*

D. Editing the Second Draft

After you have written a second draft, proofread your work for any errors and correct them. These guidelines and exercises should help.

1. Expressing Another Person's Opinion

When writing a summary, it is necessary to express another person's opinion in your own words. This is known as paraphrasing. Whenever you paraphrase, be sure to cite the source of the information to avoid plagiarism.

USE A VARIETY OF EXPRESSIONS TO CITE SOURCES

according to [the author], . . .
[the author] feels/says/maintains/believes/states . . .
[the author] is trying to express . . .
[the author] wants to show us . . .

QUOTE

"We are going from a period of time where people had babies to where people make babies."
                                                    McGee, author of <u>The Perfect Baby</u>

SUMMARY

McGee, the author of <u>The Perfect Baby</u>, believes that very soon people will be able to choose the traits that their children will have.

When paraphrasing, you should also use synonyms for key nouns and verbs:
"... research is very **important** to ..."   ... this **vital** research will show ...
                QUOTE   PARAPHRASE

And vary your sentence structure
"Researchers carried out studies . . ."   Studies were performed by . . .
        QUOTE (ACTIVE VOICE)   PARAPHRASE (PASSIVE VOICE)

In your notebook, paraphrase these quotes in a summary. Be sure to cite the source and explain it in your own words. Then respond to the quote by writing your opinion. Discuss your summaries and responses with a partner.

1. "We are going from a period of time where people had babies to where people make babies."   McGee, author of *The Perfect Baby*

Summary: McGee, the author of <u>The Perfect Baby</u>, believes that very soon people will be able to choose the traits that their children will have.

Response: If this is true, the future will be wonderful because every baby will be beautiful, smart, and healthy.

2. "When you see something that is technologically sweet, you go ahead and do it."

Robert Oppenheimer, one of the creators of the atomic bomb

3. "Each human life is unique, born of a miracle that reaches beyond laboratory science. I believe we must respect this profound gift and resist the temptation to replicate ourselves."

Bill Clinton, former president of the United States

4. Cloning is ". . . a matter far too important to be left solely in the hands of the scientific and medical communities."

Dr. James Watson, Nobel Prize winner, genetic engineer, and one of the scientists who discovered the structure of DNA

2. Subject-Verb Agreement

If the subject of a sentence is singular, the verb form must also be singular. If the subject is plural, the verb form must be plural.

The Scottish researchers <u>were trying</u> to do something less controversial.

PLURAL SUBJECT   PLURAL VERB

The author <u>feels</u> that people are more than their genes.

SINGULAR   SINGULAR
SUBJECT   VERB

Cloning humans <u>raises</u> frightening scenarios.

SINGULAR   SINGULAR
SUBJECT   VERB

Note that a subject can be a gerund like "cloning humans," which is considered a singular idea. Since gerunds are considered singular, they take a singular verb.

Read these paragraphs on the legal arguments about cloning and look for errors in subject-verb agreement. Cross out the incorrect verb forms and write your corrections above them. There are 13 errors in total. All of the verbs are in the active or passive present tense.

Some people feel that scientific experiments ~~is~~ *are* protected by the First

Amendment to the United States Constitution. This amendment protect the

right of freedom of speech. A legal scholar from the University of Chicago

argue that this is a realistic constitutional claim. He maintain that the

continued

founding fathers were concerned with scientific and academic freedom, and the members of the Supreme Court today also has a high regard for it.

Arguments in favor of defending research rights by using the First Amendment is complex. One of the many legal scholars involved say that raising questions that challenges and explores cultural norms are exactly the kind of research the founding fathers wanted to encourage.

According to legal scholars, the government can restrict research only if the studies in question threatens national security or public health. While releasing smallpox into the air to see how it spreads are clearly a threat and could be banned, conducting stem cell experiments do not present a clear danger to public health or security.

E. Preparing the Final Draft

Reread your second draft and correct any errors you find. Put a (✓) in each space as you edit for these points. Then write your corrected final version.

> **CHECKLIST FOR EDITING THE SECOND DRAFT**
>
> _____ **paraphrasing**
>
> _____ **subject-verb agreement**

 # V Additional Writing Opportunities

Write about one of the following topics.

1. According to journalist George Seldes, "All great ideas are controversial, or have been at one time." What do you think Seldes means by this? How do you feel about it? Write an essay in which you respond to this quote. Use examples to support your opinions.

2. Should we allow scientists to use cloning to try to develop cures for specific diseases, for example Alzheimer's Disease? Write a letter to the editor of your local newspaper that states your position on this subject.

3. "Technological possibilities are irresistible to man," said John von Neumann, one of the creators of the atom bomb. "If man can go to the moon, he will." What point is von Neumann trying to make? Do you agree or disagree? Write an essay expressing how you feel about this statement. Be sure to give examples to support your opinions.

4. Should parents be allowed to choose the genetic traits, such as gender, eye color, or future IQ, of their unborn child? How about personality traits, talents, or resistance to certain diseases? Write an essay that discusses how you feel about creating the "perfect baby." What are the advantages and disadvantages?

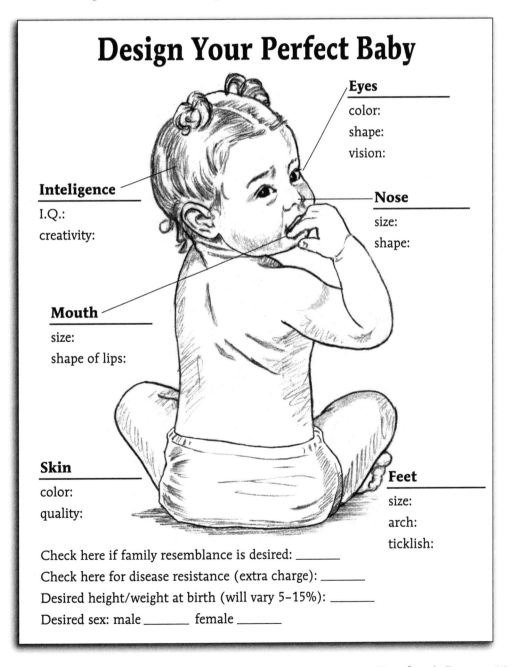

Design Your Perfect Baby

Eyes _____
color:
shape:
vision:

Inteligence _____
I.Q.:
creativity:

Nose _____
size:
shape:

Mouth _____
size:
shape of lips:

Skin _____
color:
quality:

Feet _____
size:
arch:
ticklish:

Check here if family resemblance is desired: _____
Check here for disease resistance (extra charge): _____
Desired height/weight at birth (will vary 5–15%): _____
Desired sex: male _____ female _____

CHERRIES FOR MY GRANDMA

WRITING A DESCRIPTIVE ESSAY

In this unit you will practice:
- analyzing essay organization
- writing detailed examples as support
- using a summary as an introduction

Editing focus:
- adjective clauses
- habitual past: *would* vs. *used to*

 ## Fluency Practice: Freewriting

Look at the picture. What do you think the relationship is between these people? How do they influence each other? Who had the most influence on you as a child? What did you do together?

Write for ten minutes. Try to express yourself as well as you can. Don't worry about mistakes. Share your writing with a partner.

21

II ▸ Reading for Writing

This reading is adapted from an acceptance speech for an award for "contributions to the human condition." The author, Geoffrey Canada, was president of the Rheedlen Centers for Children and Families in New York City at the time of the award. Rheedlen, now called The Harlem Children's Zone, is a community-based, not-for-profit organization offering educational, social, and employment services for poor families.

CHERRIES FOR MY GRANDMA

I   I grew up poor in the Bronx. My mother raised my three brothers and me by herself. When she couldn't find work, we went on welfare.[1] When she could find work, it was in jobs that paid women so little money that we couldn't tell the difference between welfare and work except that our mother wasn't home when she was working. People talk about poverty and the poor like it's so easy to not be poor. But I know a different story. It takes great sacrifice and talent to work your way out of poverty.

II   My mother used to make all of her own clothes. You couldn't raise four boys on her salary and afford to buy dresses to wear to work. When we were young, she used to make our clothes, cut our hair and make toys for us out of cereal boxes. All her life she sacrificed for us. She put off getting her college degree and her master's degree until we were grown and on our own.

III   And you know what? We hated being poor. We loved our mother but we ruined her Christmas every year with our tears of disappointment at not getting exactly what we wanted. I couldn't help but be angry when my shoes had holes in them and there was no money to buy new ones. And I couldn't help but stare angrily when I needed money to go on a school trip and there wasn't any money to be had.

IV   And while there was much love in our family, being poor strained[2] our loving bonds. We had to blame someone, and my mother was the only target. And here she was giving up all she had for us, going without lunch, without movies and nights out, walking 10 blocks to the train because she couldn't afford to pay the 15 cents extra to take the bus. And she would come home to four boys with their hands out, angry because we wanted something, needed something she could not give.

V   There are some Americans who think poverty stems from[3] a lack of values and determination. But you can work hard all your life, have impeccable[4] values and still be poor. My grandfather was the pastor of Mount Pleasant Baptist Church in Harlem. My grandmother was a Christian woman. They were hard-working, moral people. They were poor.

1. *welfare:* government system of aid for the poor
2. *strained:* to injure by excessive pressure
3. *stems from:* comes from
4. *impeccable:* without faults; flawless

VI   I lived with my grandparents during my high school years. My grandmother worked all her life: caring for other people's children, selling baked goods or beauty products, doing whatever she could do to help bring money into the house. She was a beautiful woman, kind and intelligent. She was determined to save my soul.[5]

VII   I was a wild and reckless adolescent whose soul was indeed in danger. And I fell in love with my grandmother. A deep love that any of us would develop if an angel came into our lives. The more time I spent with her, the more I loved her. She cooled my hot temper and anger over being poor, and she showed me there was dignity[6] even in poverty.

VIII In all the years I knew her, she was never able to afford material things that others took for granted.[7] She worked very hard but never could afford anything of luxury.[8] She taught me how one could enjoy a deep spiritual love of life that was not tied to material things. This is a tough lesson to teach in a country that places so much value on materialism.

IX   But each summer my grandmother and I would secretly plan to indulge[9] her one vice[10]: cherries. She loved cherries. Two or three times a week when my grandfather was at work, I would walk the mile to the supermarket and buy half a pound of cherries. My grandmother and I would eat them secretly because my grandfather would have had a fit[11] if he'd known we spent an extra dollar a week on them.

X   My summers with my grandmother were measured by how good the cherries were that year. It was our little secret. And I was amazed at how much she loved cherries, and how expensive cherries were. Later when I went off to Bowdoin College in Brunswick, Maine, I would sit in my room and think about how much my mother and grandmother had sacrificed for me to be in college.

XI   I would fantasize about how when I graduated and got a good job, the first thing I would buy with my first check in August would be a whole crate of cherries. It would have to be August because our cherry summers taught us that August cherries were the sweetest. I would dream of wrapping the crate up in gift paper, putting a bow on it and presenting it to Grandma. And many a night I would go to sleep in the cold winter Maine nights warmed by the vision of my grandmother's excitement when I brought her this small treasure.

continued

5. *save a soul:* help become a better person
6. *dignity:* the quality of being worthy, honored or esteemed
7. *take for granted:* assume something is deserved
8. *luxury:* great ease or comfort; rich surroundings
9. *indulge:* give in to something or someone
10. *vice:* a moral fault or failing
11. *have a fit:* get angry

XII   Grandma died during my sophomore year. I never got to give her all the cherries she could eat. And if you want my opinion, the summer of 1971, the last summer she was alive, was really the last great summer for cherries.

XIII   Poverty is tough on families in many ways. It's not quite as simple to get out of as people make out. We must be careful to make sure we build ladders so children and their families can climb out of poverty. It's not an easy climb. You can climb all your life and never make it out.

XIV   Grandma, who sacrificed so much for all of us, I just want to say I know that in all I've been acknowledged for,[12] I still haven't reached the level of love and compassion that you tried to teach me. I think you accomplished your goal: you saved my soul. And I hope they let me bring gifts to Heaven. You'll know what's in the box.

---

12. *be acknowledged for:* be recognized and honored for

A. General Understanding

1. Understanding the Reading

Do the exercises below. Then share your answers with a partner. For each exercise more than one answer may be correct.

1. Who does the author, Geoffrey Canada, discuss in this article?

    a. his grandmother   c. his father   e. his friend
    b. his grandfather   d. his mother

2. There are several themes in the article. Write the paragraph numbers where Canada discusses each theme.

_____ a. how difficult it is to get an education when you are poor

_____ b. his love for his grandmother

_____ c. how he didn't appreciate his mother

_____ d. how difficult it is to climb out of poverty

3. In your opinion, why does Canada use his personal relationships in this story? Be prepared to discuss why you feel this way.

_____ a. to honor them

_____ b. to illustrate how difficult it is to climb out of poverty

_____ c. to serve as an example of how we can help each other

_____ d. to show the readers that poverty is personal

_____ e. to illustrate how difficult it is to live in a materialistic culture

2. What Do You Think?

Answer these questions on your own. You may have to infer the answers from what you read. Then share your answers with a partner.

1. How does Canada feel about the people who influenced his life? Explain why he feels this way.

   His mother: _____

   _____

   His grandmother: _____

   _____

   His grandfather: _____

   _____

2. What lessons did Canada's grandmother teach him? What do you think about them?

   _____

   _____

3. What lessons did Canada's mother teach him? What do you think about them?

   _____

   _____

4. What lessons does society need to learn, according to Canada? What do you think about them?

   _____

   _____

5. What's in the box that Canada wants to bring to heaven? What are some things that this gift could symbolize?

   _____

   _____

B. Working with Language

1. Identifying Synonyms

Circle all possible synonyms (words with similar meaning) for each bold word. Compare your answers with a partner.

1. **sacrifice**	care about	(give up)	(do without)
2. **strain**	injure	harm	differentiate
3. **dignity**	independence	value	honor
4. **determined**	firm	intelligent	indecisive
5. **reckless**	strict	careless	irresponsible
6. **fantasize**	dream	imagine	remember
7. **tough**	easygoing	strong	difficult
8. **compassion**	pity	love	concern
9. **materialistic**	greedy	worldly	spiritual
10. **put off**	avoid	delay	postpone

2. Word Forms

Fill in the chart with the missing forms of the words. Use a dictionary, if necessary.

	Noun	Verb	Adjective	Adverb
1.		sacrifice	1. 2.	——
2.	dignity			——
3.	target			——
4.			determined	——
5.		——	reckless	
6.		——	compassionate	
7.		——	materialistic	
8.		fanatisize		——
9.			tough	
10.		strain		——

3. Describing Characters

Read the list of adjectives. Write each adjective next to the person or people it could be used to describe in "Cherries for My Grandma."

beautiful	hard-working	moral	talented
compassionate	intelligent	poor	tough
determined	kind	reckless	
dignified	materialistic	sacrificing	

Geoffrey Canada: _____

His mother: _____

His grandmother: _____

His grandfather: _____

4. Writing a Summary

In your notebook, write a summary of "Cherries for My Grandma" using some of the words in this section.

III Prewriting Activities

This excerpt is from an essay by Gary Soto, poet and essayist, in which he fondly remembers his grandfather and the time they spent together. Soto uses very few adjectives to describe his grandfather, but his detailed descriptions of the things around his grandfather help communicate his grandfather's character.

MY GRANDFATHER

Grandfather believed a well-rooted tree was the color of money. His money he kept hidden behind portraits of sons and daughters or taped behind the calendar of an Aztec warrior. He tucked it into the sofa, his shoes and slippers, and into the tight-lipped pockets of his suits. He kept it in his soft brown wallet that was machine tooled with "Mexico" and a campesino[1] and donkey climbing a hill. He had climbed, too, out of Mexico, settled in Fresno and worked thirty years at the Sun Maid Raisin factory, first as a packer and later, when he was old, as a watchman with a large clock on his belt.

continued

---

1. *campesino:* a Mexican farmer

10 After work, he sat in the backyard under the trees, watching the water gurgle[2] in the rose bushes that ran along the fence. A lemon tree hovered[3] over the clothesline. Two orange trees stood near the alley. His favorite tree, the avocado, which had started in a jam jar from a seed and three toothpicks lanced in its sides, rarely bore fruit. He said it was the wind's
15 fault and the mayor's, who allowed office buildings so high that the haze of pollen[4] from the countryside could never find its way into the city. He sulked[5] about this. He said that in Mexico buildings only grew so tall. You could see the moon at night, and the stars were clear points all the way to the horizon. And wind reached all the way to the sea, which was blue and
20 clean, unlike the oily water sloshing against a San Francisco pier.

After ten years, the first avocado hung on a branch, but the meat was spotted with black, an omen, Grandfather thought, a warning to keep an eye on the living. Five years later, another avocado hung on a branch, larger than the first and edible[6] when crushed with a fork into a heated
25 tortilla. Grandfather sprinkled it with salt and spiced it with a river of chile.

"It's good," he said, and let me taste.

I took a big bite, waved a hand over my tongue, and ran for the garden hose gurgling in the rose bushes. I drank long and deep, and later ate the smile from an ice-cold watermelon.

---

2. *gurgle:* to make a sound like a liquid flowing unevenly
3. *hovered:* remained hanging over
4. *pollen:* a mass of microspores of seeds, usually appearing as dust
5. *sulked:* refused to speak because of anger or displeasure
6. *edible:* able to be eaten

A. Recognizing Detailed Descriptions

Read each adjective and decide whether it could be used to describe Soto's grandfather. Write the line numbers where the support for your choices can be found.

_____ a. homesick   _____ i. reckless

_____ b. ambitious   _____ j. a lover of beauty

_____ c. materialistic   _____ k. hardworking

_____ d. irrational   _____ l. intelligent

_____ e. shy   _____ m. distrustful

_____ f. talkative   _____ n. curious

_____ g. dignified   _____ o. superstitious

_____ h. poor

In Soto's essay, he appeals to all the senses: seeing, hearing, touching, tasting, and smelling. In your notebook, write as many examples as you can find for each sense. Compare your answers with a partner.

In "…watching the water gurgle in the rose bushes that ran along the fence," Soto appeals to the senses of seeing, hearing, and smelling (the scent of the rosebushes).

B. Writing Detailed Descriptions

Think of a person who has influenced you. In your notebook, write at least three characteristics of the person. Then write a detailed memory to describe each characteristic. Remember to appeal to the senses in your descriptions. Share your descriptions with a partner.

My grandmother

She was a good cook.

For every holiday, she prepared special food. For Christmas, she made wine cookies. Into a white mound of flour, she cupped a hole in the center, which reminded me of the volcanoes we studied in school. Then she poured warmed wine into the opening and kneaded the dough on the scarred wooden board my grandfather had made for her.

C. Open for Discussion

Read the questions. Write a response to one or two of the questions in your notebook. Then discuss your responses in a small group.

1. Can a short encounter with someone have as great an impact as a long-term relationship? If so, give an example and explain. If not, why not?

2. Can the impact one person has on another person change? Can a good influence become a bad one? How?

3. What does the following quote mean? Do you agree with it? Give personal examples to support your opinions.

   > *Whatever you may be sure of, be sure of this—that you are dreadfully like other people.*
   > James Russell Lowell (1819–1891)

4. According to Geoffrey Canada, "There are some Americans who think poverty stems from a lack of values and determination." What do you think? Are people poor because of their own actions or character?

5. What does a person need in order to climb out of poverty? How should the government of a country help the poor? How important is family in overcoming poverty?

Structured Writing Focus

Write a five-paragraph descriptive essay about a childhood relationship with a person who has had a powerful influence over you. Give specific examples and detailed descriptions of things you did together and conversations you had. Show how this relationship helped you to become the person you are today.

ALTERNATIVE TASK: Write a five-paragraph summary and response essay. In the introductory paragraph, summarize the personal lessons Geoffrey Canada learned from his grandmother in "Cherries for My Grandma." Write a response that shows at least three ways that you agree or disagree with Canada. You can base your response on your own experience, your reading, or your opinion.

A. Starting to Write

Brainstorming

In your notebook, write notes on these questions to help you with your essay.

FOR THE MAIN TASK

Describe an important person from your childhood. Who is the person that had the most influence over you in your childhood? What did you like or dislike about this person? What kinds of things did you do together? Talk about? Write down several examples. Do your examples appeal to different senses? How did this person help or teach you? Do you still think about this person? In what situations?

FOR THE ALTERNATIVE TASK

Look back at your answers to Exercise 2 on page 25 and the summary you wrote for Exercise 4 on page 27. How can you use this material in your essay?

B. Preparing the First Draft

1. Analyzing Essay Structure

An essay can be divided into three parts: the **introduction**, the **body**, and the **conclusion**.

The first paragraph of an essay is the **introduction**.

The introduction moves from the general to the specific. It often begins with a hook to capture the reader's attention. The hook is followed by some *general statements* on a topic. The introduction must also include a main idea, known as a *thesis statement*.

The **body of an essay** may consist of several paragraphs and includes information that supports the thesis statement.
This information may be in the form of *Statistics, Anecdotes, Facts, Examples*, or *Reasons* (SAFER).

The last paragraph of an essay is the **conclusion**.

The conclusion begins with a *restatement* of the thesis statement. It often sums up important arguments, gives advice or an opinion, and leaves the reader with something to think about. The conclusion should contain key words and phrases from the introduction and body to unify the essay.

Read the student's first draft and identify the parts of the essay: introduction, body paragraphs, and conclusion. When you have finished, answer the questions on the next page in your notebook and compare your answers with a partner's.

STUDENT ESSAY FIRST DRAFT

My Little Aunt

a. _____

I was the oldest kid in my family with three siblings. Unlike most other kids who were born as the first child, I never longed for an older sibling. The reason was clear, because I practically had one. It was my aunt, my mother's little sister. She was only ten years older than I so she was like a big sister rather than an aunt. She had spent all her summer and winter vacations, from her elementary school to college, with us in Seoul. Even after she got her job, she would come and spend time with us whenever she had time to do so. I never realized until I became a grown-up myself how much influence she had on me.

b. _____

I remember how much I wanted to grow up fast so that I could be like her. Her snow-white skin and elegant look would make every head turn whenever we went out, and this made me very proud. She was the one who taught me the "Dos and Don'ts" of fashion and how to draw a perfect eye line (which, unfortunately, I still can't do right today).

continued

Cherries for My Grandma 31

c. _____

As I grew older, I began to suspect that it was illegal for a girl to think about things other than fashion and beauty. All the time I was admiring her, the little devil in me was judging her, telling myself this and that. I grew tired of her endless 'fashion talk.' To me, it seemed time-consuming, not-so-constructive, even worthless. Nevertheless, I would impress my friends with all the fashion and beauty tips my aunt had passed down to me. My adolescent years were full of conflict between the longing to be like her and my refusal to become one of her kind.

d. _____

It was only when I grew much older and got married that I came to realize how lucky I am to have an aunt who can have a good conversation with me. Nowadays, she gladly advises me, not only on fashion and beauty, but also on everything from nursing to married life. She not only made my childhood happy, but also made my whole life richer by becoming my mentor. Come what may, I know there's always someone that I can count on. My little aunt will always be there, ten years ahead of me.

1. Does the first sentence have a hook for the reader? How can the writer make the first sentence more interesting?

2. Is there a *thesis statement*—one sentence that states the main idea of the essay? Which sentence is it? How could it be better?

3. Does each body paragraph begin with a *topic sentence*—the main idea of the paragraph? Does each body paragraph make one point?

4. In her introduction, the writer says that her aunt influenced her a lot. What support is given for this idea in body paragraph 1?

5. What details could be added to the description of the main character: the aunt's appearance, the fashion advice she gave? What would the reader like to know so that the aunt comes alive in the description?

6. What senses does the writer appeal to in her descriptions? How can she improve her descriptions?

7. Do the paragraphs follow logically? In the third paragraph, the writer says she was critical of her aunt. In the last paragraph, she talks about her admiration for her aunt. What information is missing?

8. Does the conclusion restate the thesis and sum up the support? Does she unify the essay in any way?

9. Can you find any errors in essay form? What are they?

Now read this second draft of the student essay. Answer the questions that follow. Then compare your answers with those of your classmates and your teacher.

STUDENT ESSAY SECOND DRAFT

Ten Years Ahead of Me

Unlike most other kids who were born the first child, I never longed for an older sibling. The reason was clear: I practically had one. It was my aunt, my mother's little sister. I called her "My Little Aunt." She was only ten years older than I, so she was like a big sister rather than an aunt. She had spent all her summer and winter vacations, from elementary school to college, with us in Seoul. Even after she got her job, she would come and spend time with us whenever she had time to do so. I never realized until I became a grown-up myself how much influence my aunt had on me. She was an idol to me in childhood, someone to rebel against in my teenage years, and a role model in my career.

When I was a child, I was fascinated by everything about her. I remember how much I longed to have long, slim fingers like hers and how much I wanted to grow up fast so that I could treat my hair the way she treated hers. Even her dreamy eyes and slightly curled-up nose, which my mother used to make fun of, seemed gorgeous to me. Her snow-white skin and elegant look would make every head turn whenever we went out, and this made me very proud. Non-no (a Japanese fashion magazine) and Vogue were her Bible. "It's almost a sin to not match your shoes and bag," she would say. When we were watching a TV show together, she would point to the screen with her long, slender finger and say, "See? She shouldn't wear a full skirt with a blazer." She was the one who told me why it is so important for a classy woman to own a Louis Vuitton Speedy. She was the one who taught me all the "Dos and Don'ts" of fashion and how to draw a perfect eye line (which, unfortunately, I still can't do right today).

As I grew older, I began to resent that it seemed forbidden for a girl to think about things other than fashion and beauty matters. All the time I was admiring her, the little devil in me was judging her, whispering this and that. I grew tired of her endless 'fashion talks.' To me it seemed time-consuming, not-so-constructive, even worthless. When I got older, I used to insult her with comments like "Auntie, is there anything you can think of other than shoes and bags?" or "This is all so foolish. I'd rather talk about something worth talking about." Nevertheless, I would impress my peers with all the fashion and beauty tips my aunt had passed down to me. My adolescent years were full of conflict between the longing to be like her and my refusal to become one of her kind.

continued

Cherries for My Grandma   33

It came as rather a surprise when my aunt went to college and started to study Special Education. It was even more surprising when she actually became a Special Education teacher for physically handicapped children. My mother said auntie's not-so-high test scores forced her to choose the college she went to as well as her major. I speculated that she had finally grown tired of stacking shoes and bags in her wardrobe, and now wanted to play the noble Ms. Sullivan from The Miracle Worker. Despite our unkind theories, she seemed to really enjoy teaching and working with handicapped children. She didn't lose her elegance and sense of style, but now she would talk about how happy she was being with children and how she was learning the meaning of life from her students. She did such a good job convincing me that I actually went to college to study Special Education myself!

"My little aunt" not only made my childhood happier, she also made my whole life richer by becoming my life's mentor. When I grew much older and got married, I finally realized how lucky I am to have an aunt I can talk to. Nowadays our conversations are not only on fashion and beauty, but on everything from married life to our careers. Come what may, I know there's always someone that I can count on. My little aunt will always be there, ten years ahead of me.

1. How has the writer improved the hook? Why is it more interesting now?

2. Does the thesis statement prepare the reader for the points the writer plans to make in the body paragraphs? How?

3. What examples and detailed descriptions have been added to the body paragraphs? How many senses does the writer appeal to? Find examples in the essay.

4. How does the addition of the fourth paragraph improve the essay?

5. Which title is more interesting? Why?

6. Does the conclusion reflect the thesis statement and unify the essay?

7. In what ways is the essay format different? Is it better? Why or why not?

2. Practice with Hooks

Just as a fisherman uses a hook to catch a fish, the beginning sentences of an essay often function as a hook to capture the reader's attention. There are many ways you can do this.

---

a. **Begin with a question.** The reader will want to respond to the question. *How many days a year did you spend with your grandmother?*

b. **Begin with a famous quote or some dialogue.**
You can't judge a book by its cover. I learned this the summer I turned sixteen.

c. **Use descriptive language related to the topic.**
I was just a little girl. My whole world was made up of my swing hanging above the grass, my best friend next door, and the chocolate I would let melt on the floor behind the living room sofa.

d. **Begin with clues to arouse interest in the main topic.**
I grew up poor in the Bronx. My mother raised my three brothers and me by herself.

Check the sentences that would make the best hooks for an essay about a person who has influenced your life. Explain your choices in your notebook and share them with the class.

_____ 1. Many people have been influenced by someone special when they were young.

This is not a very interesting hook. It doesn't use descriptive language, a question or a quote.

✓ 2. When I was young, I was not a well-behaved child.

This is an interesting hook. I want to know how the writer misbehaved. I can identify with him because I got in trouble when I was young, too.

_____ 3. "I want to leave home. Now!"

_____ 4. The person who had the most powerful influence over me in my childhood was my first English teacher.

_____ 5. Have you ever been called "stupid" in class?

_____ 6. Many people have come in and out of my life.

_____ 7. He didn't even know my name when he passed away.

3. Practice with Thesis Statements

The **thesis statement** tells the reader what the essay is going to be about—the topic of the essay. It also tells the reader how the author thinks or feels about the topic—the controlling idea. In a **descriptive essay**, thesis statements often give this information indirectly. Sometimes, a thesis statement will also include information about the organization of the body of an essay.

Note: A thesis statement is similar to the topic sentence of a paragraph. However, the topic sentence comes at the beginning of a paragraph, while a thesis statement should come at the end of the first paragraph in an essay.

Check the sentences that would make a good thesis statement for an essay about a person who has influenced your life. Explain your choices in your notebook and share them with the class.

__✓__ 1. It was my mom who taught me not to give up on my dreams.

This is a good thesis statement because it tells us who the essay is about and how the author feels about her. It gives us an idea about how his mother influenced him. It also avoids a direct response such as "The person who influenced me the most is . . ."

_____ 2. I never understood why so many people enjoyed English class.

_____ 3. His love for us was symbolized by the different flowers in that bouquet.

_____ 4. This was because she was educated in the old-fashioned way.

_____ 5. My grandfather has influenced me a lot and has taught me many important lessons.

_____ 6. The only person I felt confident with was Eun Jung, who was my playmate, my best friend, and my inspiration.

_____ 7. In my case, my mother highly influenced my character through an incident with a match.

_____ 8. Geoffrey Canada's grandmother taught him spiritual values, self-control, and the meaning of dignity; these are essential lessons for all people.

4. Using a Summary as an Introduction

Students are often asked to summarize a reading and then use it to introduce their own essay. Read this summary of the Soto essay that you read on pages 27–28. Then answer the questions.

In "My Grandfather," Gary Soto movingly describes his grandfather, using a series of images to reveal his grandfather's character. His grandfather moved from Mexico to the United States and we sense that he is still homesick for his native country. He was a poor, but proud man who worked hard all his life. He is a lover of beauty, who tenderly cares for his garden. His love for his grandson is clear from the conversations Soto describes. Soto's admiration for his grandfather is obvious. The lessons he learned from him are about hard work, a love of beauty, and the importance of family. In my life, it was a stranger who taught me these lessons.

1. What important information is included in the first sentence? What type of hook does the writer use?

2. Which three themes from the essay does this summary mention?

3. How does the summary conclude? Which sentence makes a transition from Soto's article to the new topic?

5. Supporting Your Opinions with Detailed Examples

Support your opinions with some kind of proof in the body of your essay or your readers have no reason to believe you. In a descriptive essay, you will most likely use examples and anecdotes as support.

Look back at the essay by Geoffrey Canada on pages 22–24. He uses personal examples to support his opinions. Read these opinions about the Canada essay. Then write down the support he offers for these opinions in your notebook. If there is no support for an opinion, say so.

1. His grandparents were poor, but they were not lazy.

His grandfather was the pastor of a church. His grandmother worked all her life. She cared for children, sold baked goods and beauty products, and did other jobs to earn money. They were hard-working people.

2. His mother sacrificed many things for him.

3. He loved his mother.

4. His grandmother had a profound influence over him.

5. He loved his grandmother.

6. He was a reckless adolescent.

6. Organizing Your Essay

Study this block diagram of a five-paragraph essay to plan a first draft of your essay. In your notebook, draw your own diagram and write your notes in each of its sections.

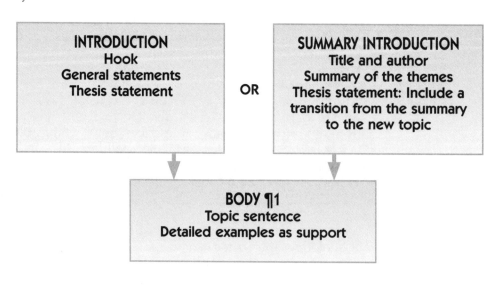

INTRODUCTION
Hook
General statements
Thesis statement

OR

SUMMARY INTRODUCTION
Title and author
Summary of the themes
Thesis statement: Include a
transition from the summary
to the new topic

BODY ¶1
Topic sentence
Detailed examples as support

BODY ¶2
Topic sentence
Detailed examples as support

BODY ¶3
Topic sentence
Detailed examples as support

CONCLUSION
Restatement of thesis
Refer back to hook to unify essay

*Write a **first draft** of your essay. Try to use some of the vocabulary and structures in this unit.*

C. Revising the First Draft

When you have finished writing your first draft, read it to a partner.

CHECKLIST FOR REVISING THE FIRST DRAFT

When you listen to your partner's essay and when you discuss your own, keep these questions in mind:

1. Does your hook capture the reader's attention?

2. Does your thesis statement make it clear who or what you are talking about and how you feel about this subject?

3. Are there enough examples in the body of your essay to support your thesis?

4. Can your reader imagine what you are describing? How many senses do your examples appeal to?

5. Does the first sentence of your conclusion restate your thesis?

If you are using a summary introduction, keep these additional questions in mind:

1. Do you mention the title and author in your first sentence?

2. Do you summarize the main themes of the reading?

3. Does your thesis explain the relationship between the reading and your essay?

After discussing your essay with your partner, you may want to change your hook and thesis statement. You might also want to add more detailed examples as support in the body of your essay.

*Now write a **second draft** that includes all of your additions and deletions.*

D. Editing the Second Draft

After you have written a second draft, proofread your work for any errors and correct them. These guidelines and exercises should help.

1. Adjective Clauses: Restrictive and Nonrestrictive

Vary the length of your sentences to make them more interesting. You can write longer, more complex sentences by using adjective clauses. Adjective clauses are also useful in descriptions. There are two types of adjective clauses.

A **restrictive** adjective clause identifies the noun it describes:

The person **who influenced me the most** is my father.

That was the day **that my childhood ended**.

The town **where she grew up** was big and exciting.

The town **in which she grew up** was big and exciting.*

A **nonrestrictive** adjective clause gives additional information about the noun it describes. It is not essential to the sentence. Use commas to set off nonrestrictive clauses:

My grandfather, **who was almost 70**, liked to tell people that he was 75.

Twilight, **when the lights came on and life slowed down**, was my favorite time of day.

He told me he was born in Tokyo, **which surprised me**.

This book, **in which everyone's name and birthday were written**, sat proudly on my grandmother's shelf.

*In current American English, *that* is used to introduce restrictive clauses and *which* is used to introduce nonrestrictive clauses. It is possible, however, to use preposition + *which* to introduce restrictive clauses.

Study these sentences from Gary Soto's essay. Why do you think the writer used a restrictive or nonrestrictive clause in each case? Discuss your ideas with a partner.

He kept his money in a brown wallet **that was machine tooled with "Mexico" and a campesino and donkey climbing a hill**.

His favorite tree, the avocado, **which had started in a jam jar from a seed and three toothpicks lanced in its sides**, rarely bore fruit.

Five years later, another avocado hung on a branch, larger than the first and edible **when crushed with a fork into a heated tortilla**.

Choose five nouns from your essay that do not have an adjective clause. Write them in the left hand column in the chart. Then, in the right hand column, write some information about each noun.

Noun	Information about noun
the sea	blue and clean as the sky bare as the surface of the moon like a sleeping giant
1.	
2.	
3.	
4.	
5.	

In your notebook, write full sentences with restrictive or nonrestrictive clauses based on the chart above. Be sure to add commas for the nonrestrictive clauses. Try to use the sentences in your essay.

The sea, which was as blue as the sky, rocked me to sleep as our boat sailed farther away from shore.

2. Habitual Past: *used to* vs *would*

Both *used to* and *would* can be used with the simple form of a verb to express **repeated actions in the past**. Try to use both expressions to add variety to your writing about past events.

Used to suggests a comparison between the past and the present, even if the present is not specifically mentioned. Something was true or usual in the past but is not true or usual now.

My family **used to live** in a small town. (but now we live in a city)
She **used to work** nights. (but now she doesn't)
They **didn't use to enjoy** visiting their cousins.
(but now they do, or now they don't visit their cousins)

Would describes continuous actions or situations in the past. Using *would* can make your writing sound more formal and even poetic.
Every summer my family **would spend** two weeks by the sea.
We **would hide** under the covers and talk all night in whispers.

To describe a past situation, writers often define the time period with *used to*, then give the details using *would*.

Grandpa **used to take** me to the zoo on my birthday. We **would spend** the whole day looking at the animals, eating, talking, and laughing.

Study these sentences. Then answer the questions below.

a. My mother used to make our clothes for us, cut our hair and make toys for us out of cereal boxes.

b. I would dream of wrapping the crate up in gilt paper, putting a bow on it and presenting it to grandma.

c. Geoffrey Canada used to live with his grandma.

1. Which sentence(s) can be expressed by both *would* and *used to*? Why?

2. Which sentence(s) can only be expressed with *used to*? Why?

Edit the following paragraph by changing some of the simple past tenses to the habitual past, would *or* used to *plus the simple form of the verb. Use your own judgment to decide when habitual past is more appropriate. Share your answers with the class.*

When I think about my childhood, the person who comes right into my head is my Aunt Eloise. My sisters and I ~~called~~ used to call her Eloista. She was more than our nanny. My parents were hard-working people. They didn't have time to take care of us, so my aunt came to our house every morning. She brought newly baked bread for breakfast. She helped us to get ready to go to school. She prepared my lunchbox and sometimes even braided my hair. We came back from school to her delicious food. Nobody could cook like she did. She was famous for her tasty roast beef and an Italian soup called "minestrone." We had a kitten in our yard, and Aunt Eloista fed her leftover bits of the wonderful meals she cooked.

Look over the second draft of your essay. Change the simple past to the habitual past whenever possible. Share your corrections with your partner.

E. Preparing the Final Draft

Reread your second draft and correct any errors you find. Put a check (✓) in each space as you edit your essay for these points. Then write your corrected final version.

> ### CHECKLIST FOR EDITING THE SECOND DRAFT
>
> _____ **restrictive and nonrestrictive adjective clauses**
>
> _____ **habitual past with** *would* **or** *used to*

V Additional Writing Opportunities

Write about one of the following topics.

1. Choose an op-ed article from a newspaper. Summarize it in the introductory paragraph then choose one side of the issue, as Geoffrey Canada did. Try to persuade your readers of your stance on the issue by using personal examples to support your opinion.

2. Imagine that you left your native country to start life in a new country. Write a letter back home describing your new surroundings and how they have affected you.

3. Write a descriptive essay. Think of a place that has special meaning for you. Describe it and its influence on you.

4. What are the causes of poverty? How can people climb out of poverty? Write an essay in which you explain your ideas on this topic.

THREE WORLDS IN ONE

WRITING A CLASSIFICATION ESSAY

In this unit you will practice:
- determining an organizing principle for categorization
- categorizing and avoiding overlapping
- developing conclusions for classification essays

Editing focus:
- pronoun referents

 ## *I* Fluency Practice: Speaking and Freewriting

If you were asked to come up with a way of dividing the people of the world into three categories, what categories would you choose? Give examples of the members of each group. How are the members of one category different from people in the other two? Are any people left out?

Write for ten minutes. Try to express yourself as well as you can. Don't worry about mistakes. Share your writing with a partner.

II ▶ **Reading for Writing**

The following article is adapted from *The New York Times*.

SOME REFLECTIONS ON THE TECHNOLOGY OF EATING

by Bryce Nelson

All the world is divided into three parts—finger-feeders, fork-feeders, and chopstick-feeders. Why people fall into these categories, however, is a mystery. "There is no comprehensive account of the ways of putting solid food into the mouth," according to Dr. Lynn White Jr., an emeritus history
5 professor at University of California at Los Angeles and an expert on medieval technology.

The topic of the technology of eating is one that is rife with[1] dispute over the utensils used to eat food. It is also a subject loaded with chauvinism.[2] Supporters of one implement may often regard others as
10 uncivilized or even barbaric.

On Dr. White's tripartite[3] globe, fork-feeders are most common in Europe and North America, chopstick-feeders in most of Eastern Asia, and finger-feeders in much of Africa, the Middle East, Indonesia, and the Indian subcontinent. That means that fork-feeders are currently
15 outnumbered 2 to 1. Academics agree fork-users have historically been in the minority; humans have eaten with their fingers for most of the species' existence. As little as three centuries ago, most Western Europeans still used fingers, regarding the fork as decadent[4] or worse. French historian Fernand Braudel tells of one medieval preacher in Germany who
20 condemned the fork as a "diabolical[5] luxury: God would not have given us fingers if he had wished us to use such an instrument."

Forks and chopsticks became popular because they made it easier to handle hot food. Before this, people generally scooped up hot meals on flat bread. The major exception was China, where there is no evidence
25 of flat bread being eaten. According to Dr. K. C. Chang, the chairman of Harvard University's anthropology department, Chinese cuisine was characterized by small portions, which did not require cutting by a knife and fork, eaten from bowls. "There was a need for morsels[6] to be carried from a bowl to the mouth, and chopsticks met that need," he said.
30 Some of the oldest Chinese chopsticks date to 1200 B.C., Dr. Chang said. Apparently, the fork appeared on Western tables several hundred years later, but it was not readily accepted. Forks were used for many

1. *rife with:* full of something unpleasant or bad
2. *chauvinism:* belief in the superiority of one's own group
3. *tripartite:* divided into three parts
4. *decadent:* morally offensive
5. *diabolical:* wicked, devilish

years in Europe and the Near East, but only as kitchen implements, says historian Rhea Tannahill in "Food in History" (Stein and Day, 1971).

35 Though the fork was first seen in society on the tables of the rich and well born, many a crowned head,[7] including Queen Elizabeth I of England and Louis XIV of France, ate with their fingers. Indeed, Mr. Braudel states that Louis XIV ate chicken stew with his fingers and forbade the Duke of Burgundy and his brothers to use forks in his presence. History has it

40 that when Napoleon III of France, a fork man, met the Shah of Persia, a finger-feeder, the potentates[8] sharply disagreed about the proper method of bridging the gap between plate and lip. As late as 1897, Miss Tannahill writes, "sailors in the British Navy were forbidden the use of knives and forks, because they were regarded as impediments[9] to discipline and manliness."

45 Dr. White acknowledged that fork-, finger-, and chopstick-feeders can be strong defenders of their eating implements. Though they cannot document it, some scholars believe finger-feeding may be undergoing an

50 enthusiastic revival, in part because of a worldwide resurgence[10] in ethnic pride after the collapse of Western imperialism, in part because the regions and social classes with some of the

55 highest birthrates shun forks.

The exceptions are the Westernized segments of society in developing countries. Dr. Eqbal Ahmad, a social scientist from Pakistan, said upper-income

60 people in the subcontinent or in the Middle East may eat with their fingers most of the time, but often use forks on public occasions, particularly if Western guests are present.

Norge Winfred Jerome, a nutritional anthropologist at the University of

65 Kansas, School of Medicine, said upper-income people in finger-feeding areas can become more European than the Europeans in their devotion to forks. She recalled taking Egyptian guests to a Kansas City grill and finding them unable to adopt the American custom of eating barbequed ribs with their fingers. For many such Westernized people, Dr. Jerome suggested,

70 "The fork has become a status marker,[11] because it establishes distance between the food and the eater that the fingers do not."

---

6. *morsels:* small pieces of food
7. *crowned head:* king or queen
8. *potentates:* rulers with direct power over their people
9. *impediments:* obstacles; things that stand in the way of something
10. *resurgence:* return to power, life, activity
11. *status marker:* something that shows someone's economic or social level

A. General Understanding

1. Understanding the Main Ideas

Read these statements about eating utensils and decide whether they are T (true) or F (false). If a statement is false, write the correct statement in your notebook. Explain your answers to a partner.

_____ 1. Currently, there are twice as many fork-feeders in the world as chopstick- and finger-feeders combined.

_____ 2. Before the creation of forks and chopsticks, people throughout the globe used flat bread to scoop up their food.

_____ 3. Although their subjects continued to eat with their fingers, the rulers of Europe and the Middle East readily adopted the use of forks in the 17th and 18th centuries.

_____ 4. In the late 19th century, the fork was seen by officers in the British Navy as an impediment to discipline.

_____ 5. Today, forks are favored throughout the world.

2. Categorizing Information

For each eating utensil, fill in the chart based on information in the article.

Utensil	Fingers	Forks	Chopsticks
Regions in which it is used			
Reason for the preference			
Any change in preference over time, and why			

3. Summarizing Information

Now write a summary of the information in the article in your notebook. Use the chart on page 48 to help you. Share your summary with a partner.

B. Working with Language

1. Avoiding Repetition with Synonyms

Synonyms are often used to avoid repetition of words and add color and variety to the language.

Find the paragraphs listed below in the reading on pages 46–47.

1. Locate the synonyms for or alternate ways of referring to forks, fingers, and/or chopsticks.

   a. Paragraph 1:   w _____

   b. Paragraph 2:   u _____

                              i _____

   c. Paragraph 3:   i _____

2. In paragraph 4, find the synonym for *food*:

                              c _____

3. In paragraph 7, find the synonym for *revival*:

                              r _____

4. In paragraph 6, find the synonyms for *the rulers of countries*:

                              c _____

                              p _____

2. Reviewing Vocabulary

Fill in the blanks with a synonym of the words in parentheses from the box.

chauvinism	ethnic	globalization	pride
resurgence	shunned	status marker	

A Renewed Interest in Ethnic Cuisine

In the past decade or so, there has been a revival of interest in

_____ethnic_____ food. This _____ in popularity might
1. culture-based   2. return

be attributable to an increase in ethnic _____ or to the
                                          3. sense of value

fact that _____ and advances in communication have
         4. world commerce

led to an increase in interest about other cultures. While being proud

of one's native cuisine might once have been regarded as a type

of _____, today it is not only accepted, it is expected.
   5. negative nationalism

Simple foods, like rice and beans or Pad Thai noodles, which Latinos

and Thais once _____ as "peasant food," have become
               6. looked down on and avoided

increasingly popular. In fact, being knowledgeable about the cuisine

of other cultures is now seen as a trendy _____, a sign
                                          7. indication of social prestige

that a person is educated about and interested in other cultures.

C. Open for Discussion

Discuss these topics in a small group. Choose one topic and write your response to it in the form of a paragraph. Share your paragraph with a partner.

1. Think about the lives of people who live in countries where the main sources of income are industry or technology. How are their lives different from the lives of the people in societies that are predominantly agricultural?

2. Think about the way food is categorized and arranged in a supermarket. Who benefits from the existence of these categories? How? What reasons might a store manager have for changing the way the food is categorized?

3. How were the students in your school system classified? Do you think this system worked well? In what other ways could students be classified? Would these types of classifications work better? Would any of them be unfair?

4. How have eating habits changed in the last decade or so? Are people eating different foods now? Are they eating at different times? Are people eating more meals in restaurants than they used to? How are your eating habits different from those of your parents? Your grandparents?

 III Prewriting Activities

A. Chronological Classification

Alvin Toffler, a futurist, is the author of more than one dozen books, including the bestsellers *Future Shock* and *Third Wave*. In this article, Michael Finley explains Toffler's thoughts on the classification of human society through time.

> Human history can be seen as taking the shape of three great advances, or waves. The first wave of change started with the agricultural revolution of 10,000 years ago, when people moved away from nomadic wandering and hunting to find food and began to cluster into villages and develop culture. People developed a sense of cyclical time, time that repeated itself with the cycles of the moon, crops, and seasons. Everyone worked on the farm and people were generalists, able to do many types of work.
>
> *continued*

The second wave was an expression of machine muscle, the Industrial Revolution that began in the 18th century and gathered steam after America's Civil War. People began to leave the peasant culture of farming to come to work in cities, giving rise to a new factory-centered civilization. Tools became more advanced and societies produced ships, railroads, and automobiles. To accomplish this, societies invested in expensive equipment and people (labor).

Just when the machine seemed most powerful, however, there were hints of a gathering third wave, based not on muscle but on mind. It is what we call the information age. This Information Society is based on technology. It includes social, cultural, institutional, moral, and political changes resulting from the transition from a "brute force" industrial society to a "brain force" economy.

1. Understanding the Classification

Read these statements from various people about the conditions of life at different times in history. For each one, decide which "wave" the person probably belongs to according to the reading above, and give a reason for your answer.

1. "I stopped going to school when I was nine years old and went to work in the factory with my brothers."

   <u>2nd wave, people moved to cities to work in factories</u>

2. "Everyone in my family has a different schedule these days. We sometimes don't even eat dinner together."

   _____

3. "The summer was good, so we'll have plenty of food this winter. I'm happy about this because last winter was very hard."

   _____

4. "If you don't have a college degree, you can't compete in today's market."

   _____

5. "We came here last year for work in the textile mill. Our kids stay with my parents back home, and we take the train out to see them on Sunday, our day off."

   _____

6. "I'm teaching my daughter how to cook, take care of the animals, and sew clothing. Soon, she'll be ready to get married and start her own family."

   _____

2. Organizing Information

Look back at the reading on pages 51–52 and make notes in the chart below on the economics, family life / social structure, and education / intelligence in each wave of human history.

	First wave	Second wave	Third wave
Economics			
Family life and social structure			
Education and intelligence			

3. Summarizing Information

Now write a one-paragraph summary of the information in the chart. Share your summary with a partner.

IV Structured Writing Focus

Write a five-paragraph classification essay about the way the world is divided today or has been divided through history. You may use one of the categories found in the exercises in "Preparing the First Draft" or think of one of your own.

ALTERNATIVE TASK: Write a humorous essay in which you divide people, students, parents, teachers, bosses, or any other group into three categories.

As your point of departure for either task, you may use a summary of "Some Reflections on the Technology of Eating" on pages 46–47 or a summary of the information in the chart on page 53 in your introductory paragraph. See Unit 2 for more instruction.

A. Starting to Write

Brainstorming

Answer the questions to help you organize your ideas.

What are some sets of people and things?

Societies in the world

_____

_____

_____

How could each set be divided into categories?

Societies: agricultural, industrial, technological

_____

_____

_____

B. Preparing the First Draft

1. Deciding on a Principle of Organization

When you classify, you divide a group into categories with similar characteristics. You must decide on **a single principle** or basis for forming the categories. Using more than one principle of organization will result in the categories overlapping; that is, the members of one category will also fit into one or more of the other categories. This must be avoided.

Look at the following subjects and categories. Decide on the principle of organization for each and write it in the blank.

1. Governments: monarchy, democracy, dictatorship

   Governments can be categorized according to <u>who makes the decisions</u>

2. Radio stations: commercial, public, subscription

   Radio stations can be classified according to _____

3. Transportation: bicycle, car, bus

   Transportation can be classified according to _____

4. Sports: individual, partner, team

   Sports can be classified according to _____

5. Animals: herbivore, predator, omnivore

   Animals can be classified according to _____

6. Habitats: mountains, plains, shoreline

   Habitats can be classified according to _____

7. Religions: Buddhism, Christianity, Islam, Judaism

   Religions can be classified according to _____

2. Identifying Overlap

Explain the problem with the following classifications.

1. Leisure time activities: sedentary, active, creative

   Problem: *Creative activities can be sedentary or active.*

2. Hairstyles: curly, straight, fashionable

   Problem: _____

3. Films: comedies, dramas, independent

   Problem: _____

4. Cities: large, coastal, mid-size

   Problem: _____

5. Toys: boys', girls', educational

   Problem: _____

6. Types of work through history: farming, business, manufacturing

   Problem: _____

3. Analyzing a Classification Essay

INTRODUCTORY PARAGRAPH

The **introductory paragraph of a classification essay** should include three elements:

- the set of things being classified
- the three or four categories into which the set is being divided
- the significance, importance, relevance, or value of the set of things being classified.

The **thesis statement** commonly includes these elements:

By looking at world cultures in terms of fork-feeders, finger-feeders, and chopstick-feeders, we can begin to see that these groups also align in other ways related to food.

Read the introduction to the student essay, "Umbrellas and Personalities," and answer the questions that follow. Discuss your answers with a partner.

[Note, this essay is meant to be a satirical, not a serious, analysis of society.]

Umbrellas and Personalities

Thesis Statement →

There are three types of people in the world. There are those who never leave the house without an umbrella and those who never leave the house with an umbrella. In the middle, one can find a few people that sometimes, depending on the weather, take an umbrella. They are very few in number, and it is not easy to identify them. The first two groups, on the other hand, can be characterized easily. Although the distinctions between umbrella carrying habits may seem trivial, understanding these three types of people in society will help us to better understand human nature as a whole.

1. Does the writer identify the set of things that will be classified? What is it?

2. What principle of organization does the writer use?

3. Are the categories comprehensive (do they cover all members of the set)? Do the categories overlap? If so, how does the writer deal with this?

4. What is the significance or value of the classification?

5. What is this piece satirizing? Is there any real connection between umbrellas and personality? In what other ways could people try to analyze personality based on superficial observations?

BODY PARAGRAPHS

After you have clearly established your categories, **each category will become the topic of one body paragraph.** These paragraphs usually form a progression: from best to worst (or vice versa), most useful to least (or vice versa), least practical to most practical, etc.

Each body paragraph should provide details about its category. These details should clearly distinguish it from the other categories in the essay.

Each body paragraph should include a transition from the last or to the next topic. A transitional sentence can be the first or last sentence in a body paragraph or it may be an internal transition within a paragraph.

Read the next section of the student's essay and answer the questions that follow. Discuss your answers with a partner.

> The always-take-an-umbrella (ATU) personality type is quite inflexible. These people often suffer from anxiety. This is why they take an umbrella wherever they go. They cannot stand the uncertainty of the weather and want to protect themselves from unexpected showers. By carrying an umbrella, they feel that they have gained control over nature. Nature cannot get them wet. This need for control is predictably lacking in the personalities of the next umbrella behavior group.

1. What do you learn about the personality of ATU's?

2. What details does the writer use to distinguish this category?

3. Which sentence is the transitional sentence? How do you know?

In the next paragraph, the writer contrasts ATUs and NTUs (his second category).

Read the second body paragraph and answer the questions that follow. Discuss your answers with a partner.

> The never-take-an-umbrella people (NTUs) are carefree and optimistic. They always think things will work out. If they do get caught in a downpour, they take it with a smile and forget about it quickly. They don't try to control their environment; they take life as it comes. Thinking ahead is not important to NTUs. Perhaps this is why NTUs also produce more children than people in other groups. The practical concerns of life are left to those in the last category of umbrella carriers.

1. What do you learn about the personality of NTUs?

2. How does the author distinguish between ATUs and NTUs? Underline the words and phrases that show contrast with ATUs.

3. What is humorous about this paragraph?

4. Which sentence is the transitional sentence? How do you know?

In the third body paragraph, the writer discusses the third category and how it relates to the other two.

Read the third body paragraph and answer the questions that follow. Discuss your answers with a partner.

In between these two major groups, there is a third group: the sometimes-take-an-umbrella group (STU). This type of person is best characterized by an instrumental attitude to life—umbrellas are useful things to have with you on rainy days. For them, umbrellas carry absolutely no symbolic importance. STUs, however, are difficult to identify. One reason for this is that on rainy days, they may easily be mistaken for belonging to the time-honored and well-established ATU personality. Similarly, on sunny days, they may be identified as NTUs. If a way is found to explain people's behavior according to changing circumstances, we can be more successful in understanding this elusive group.

1. What do you learn about the STU category?

2. How does the author distinguish STUs from ATUs and NTUs? Underline the words and phrases that show contrast with the other categories.

3. Why does the writer save the STU group for last?

4. What is amusing about this category?

CONCLUDING PARAGRAPH

As in other essays, the **concluding paragraph of a classification essay** should begin by restating the thesis statement. It should go on to restate the main ideas of the essay. It may also

- interpret and explain the essay's main points
- explain what the thesis means for the future
- provide a solution for a problem that has been presented in the essay
- urge readers to take some action

In a small group, answer the questions to plan a concluding paragraph for the essay "Umbrellas and Personalities." Then write your own concluding paragraph.

1. How can you restate the thesis of the essay?

_____

_____

_____

2. What are the main ideas of the essay?

_____

_____

_____

3. What interpretation, explanation, or encouragement could the writer offer in the concluding paragraph?

_____

_____

_____

4. How could the writer continue the humor in the last paragraph?

_____

_____

_____

Read your paragraph aloud to your small group. When everyone has finished, discuss the good points and problems of each paragraph. Then choose one of them or compose a new one together. Share your group's concluding paragraph with the class.

4. Organizing Your Essay

Study this block diagram of a five-paragraph classification essay to plan a first draft of your essay. In your notebook, draw your own diagram and write your ideas in each of its sections.

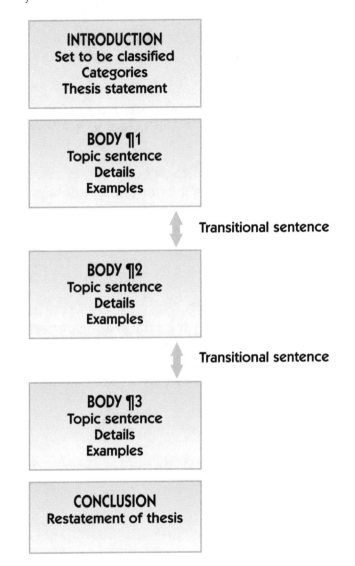

*Review your notes and consider doing some research, if needed. Then write a **first draft** of your essay. Remember to write in complete sentences.*

C. Revising the First Draft

When you have finished writing your first draft, read it to a partner.

CHECKLIST FOR REVISING THE FIRST DRAFT

When you listen to your partner's essay and when you discuss your own, keep these questions in mind:

1. Does the essay have a single principle of organization?

2. Does the essay have at least three clearly defined categories? Are the categories comprehensive? Do they overlap?

3. Does each body paragraph discuss only one category? Does it offer enough details and examples to clearly distinguish one category from the others?

4. Are there transitional sentences between the ideas?

5. Does the essay have a logical progression (from least to most, less interesting to most interesting, earliest to latest, etc.)?

6. Does the conclusion suggest a path for the future, offer a solution, interpret the main points of the essay, or urge the readers to take action?

After discussing your essay with a partner, you may want to reorganize your ideas, omit some, or add new ones.

*Now write a **second draft** that includes all of your additions and changes.*

D. Editing the Second Draft

After you have written a second draft, proofread your work for any errors and correct them. These guidelines and exercises should help.

PRONOUN REFERENTS

A writer can avoid repetition by using a **pronoun** to refer to a previously mentioned noun, noun phrase, or idea. Pronouns must agree in number with the word or words they replace.

You are familiar with the pronouns *it, he, she, they*, etc. You can use other pronouns and sentence structures involving pronouns to add complexity and sophistication to your writing.

For a singular noun or noun phrase, you can use *this* or *that*

The lecture was on the **technology of eating** [NOUN PHRASE]. I was surprised to learn that **this** [REFERENT] is a topic rife with dispute.

The **diet of an American** [NOUN PHRASE] today is more varied than **that** [REFERENT] of his parents' generation.

For a plural noun or noun phrase, you can use *these* or *those*

The **people** [NOUN] who use chopsticks or fingers outnumber **those** [REFERENT] who use forks.

City guides now list hundreds of **ethnic restaurants** [NOUN PHRASE]. Some of **these** [REFERENT] are so popular that people must make reservations well in advance.

To refer to a previous idea or assertion, you can use *this* or *that*

Some people believe that **all Chinese food is the same** [NOUN PHRASE], but **this** [REFERENT] is not the case.

(The idea that all Chinese food is the same is not the case.)

To introduce an adjective clause that further explains a noun or noun phrase, you can use *one* or *ones*

The **custom of eating with fingers** [NOUN PHRASE] is **one** [REFERENT] that some are now embracing [ADJECTIVE CLAUSE].

Some **finger-feeders** [NOUN PHRASE] have adopted forks. They are the **ones** [REFERENT] who now object most strongly to using fingers [ADJECTIVE CLAUSE].

Fill in the blanks with the appropriate pronoun: this, that, these, those, one, *or* ones.

1. While people in the West favor bread as a staple food, ___*those*___ in

   the East favor rice.

2. Evening meals in Mediterranean countries tend to be served later than

   ___*those*___ in other countries.

3. The subject of eating utensils is very controversial and is ___*one*___

   that is rife with chauvinism.

4. The food in the northern regions of India is spicier than ___*that*___ of

   the southern regions.

5. With improvements in communication and an increase in globalization, there

   has also been an increase in the cultural exchange of food, art, and design.

   ___*This*___ is one of the most welcome by-products of globalization.

6. The subject of food always inspires a great deal of discussion.

   ___*That*___ is probably because it is something everyone has

   experience with.

Edit the following passage for repetition. Which pronoun(s) can replace each underlined word or phrase? In your notebook, list all the possibilities. Then choose the one you feel works best and write it in below. Share your answers with a partner and give reasons for your choices.

Europe in the Middle Ages

Some historians focus on the topic of diet through time. They consider
~~diet~~ (it/this) an interesting way to examine the sociology and politics of past

cultures. The period of time called the Middle Ages, for example, was <u>a</u> (one/this)

<u>period of time</u> in which people lived with the threat of famine. <u>Famine</u> (it/this/one)

occurred often enough that people usually had some degree of experience

with it.

The typical daily diet of the poor was very meager. <u>The typical daily diet of the poor</u> consisted primarily of dark bread made of rye flour, soup, a few vegetables, and sometimes an egg. On festival days, there might be some meat in their wooden bowls. <u>The meat in their wooden bowls</u> came from the animals that they raised themselves. At a rich man's table, food was more plentiful. Lords and rich town dwellers' meals included plenty of meat. <u>Lords and rich town dwellers' meals</u> were eaten on metal plates.

Because there was no refrigeration, food had to be eaten quickly. Sometimes <u>the opportunity to eat food quickly</u> was not possible. To cover up any bad smell or taste, they spiced old food with cinnamon, cardamom, nutmeg, and ginger. <u>Cinnamon, cardamom, nutmeg, and ginger</u> were brought back from the Orient by soldiers and tradesmen.

In the Middle Ages, people didn't eat with spoons and forks. <u>Spoons and forks</u> came into use later. Water usually came from nearby streams or rivers. <u>The nearby streams and rivers</u> were the same <u>nearby streams and rivers</u> that people used for doing laundry, bathing, and watering animals.

E. Preparing the Final Draft

Reread your second draft and correct any errors you find. Put a check (✓) in each space as you edit for these points. Then write your corrected final version.

CHECKLIST FOR EDITING THE SECOND DRAFT

_____ avoid repetition by using pronouns where possible

_____ pronouns agree in number with the word or words they replace

V Additional Writing Opportunities

Write about one of the following topics.

1. INTERNET RESEARCH: Go online and read the study called *Blue Eyes/ Brown Eyes* that was performed by Jane Elliot, an elementary-school teacher in Riceville, Iowa, in 1968. Write an essay summarizing the study and discussing the potential dangers of classification based on physical characteristics such as race, eye color, or hair color.

2. Write an essay about different types of families. Consider nuclear families, extended families, and alternative families. In what respects are they the same? How are they different? Include a definition of family that would apply to this entire set.

3. Write an essay in which you discuss how the job of a librarian, a doctor, or an athlete has changed over three generations. How is the life and work of a doctor/librarian/athlete different now from the way it was in your parents' generation? In your grandparents' generation?

4. Write an essay in which you explore the possible ways of dividing the students in a school. Don't limit yourself to the conventional ways of making this division. Use your imagination. Which of these ways do you think might work best? Which are clearly discriminatory or unfair?

5. Write an essay about a particular kind of art form in three different areas of the world. Consider traditional music, handcrafts, pottery, or dance. In what respects are they the same? How are they different? Are they considered pure art forms in each place or do they have a different function in some places? For example, is dance part of a social or religious ritual for some societies?

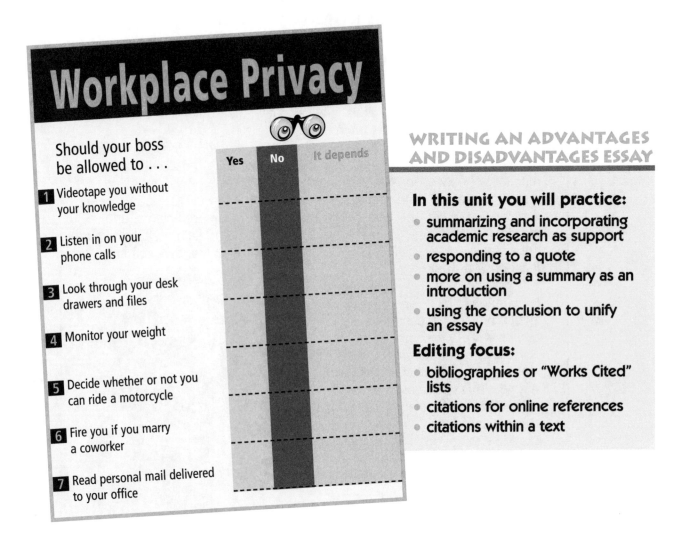

Workplace Privacy

Should your boss be allowed to . . .

	Yes	No	It depends
1 Videotape you without your knowledge			
2 Listen in on your phone calls			
3 Look through your desk drawers and files			
4 Monitor your weight			
5 Decide whether or not you can ride a motorcycle			
6 Fire you if you marry a coworker			
7 Read personal mail delivered to your office			

WRITING AN ADVANTAGES AND DISADVANTAGES ESSAY

In this unit you will practice:
- summarizing and incorporating academic research as support
- responding to a quote
- more on using a summary as an introduction
- using the conclusion to unify an essay

Editing focus:
- bibliographies or "Works Cited" lists
- citations for online references
- citations within a text

I Fluency Practice: Freewriting

Look at the poll above. Answer the questions by putting a check (✓) in the Yes, No, or It Depends column. Then choose one of the questions from the poll and write about it for ten minutes. Explain the reasons for your opinion. Try to express yourself as well as you can. Don't worry about mistakes. Share your writing with a partner.

Reading for Writing

In this article from *The New York Times* about workplace privacy, a company manager discusses why and how he monitors employee e-mail.

YOU'VE GOT INAPPROPRIATE MAIL
by Lisa Guernsey

Andrew Quinn, a systems manager at a toy company near Montreal, is starting to learn more about his fellow employees than he had ever wanted to know. He has found that one co-worker has a weakness for herbal remedies,[1] another likes jokes about women drivers and another
5 checks the lottery numbers each morning.

He knows these things because, about a month ago, Mr. Quinn installed a new piece of software on the computer network that enables him to monitor not only every Web site that his employees browse, but every e-mail message that they send or receive. With a few clicks, he can open
10 a window on a computer screen and see the senders, recipients, and subject headings of each message. Those details, he said, help him figure out exactly what is straining his e-mail server, which has been crashing at least once a week.

"This guy, he's sending e-mail to
15 his girlfriend," Mr. Quinn said as he scrolled through messages sent by employees of his company, Ritvik Toys, on a recent afternoon. "But this message here, that's for business.
20 And that one's for business, too."

To office workers elsewhere, Mr. Quinn's surveillance[2] might sound like Big Brother[3] in action. But if they think it is of no immediate concern
25 to them, they should think again. Ritvik Toys is one of hundreds of companies that are looking at workers' correspondence on a routine basis. And the number of companies
30 regularly doing so is soaring.[4]

Managers give a variety of reasons for installing such software. Some,

---

1. *herbal remedies:* preparations made from plant products, used as an alternative to medicine
2. *surveillance:* a careful watch on a person or group; supervision
3. *Big Brother:* the totalitarian figure in George Orwell's novel, *1984*
4. *soaring:* rapidly increasing

like Mr. Quinn, are on the lookout for oversize e-mail attachments that clog networks. Others seek[5] to dissuade and discourage employees from using their systems for personal activities. And others want to make sure employees are not sending messages that disturb or hurt others.

Whatever the reason, the monitoring raises ethical questions. Should managers really be peeking[6] into people's private lives like this? And what should they do with sensitive information that, if made public, could jeopardize[7] an employee's career?

Like most manufacturers, Ritvik relies more and more on the Internet to get the job done. Its 200 salaried employees now file purchase orders, do product research and make sales calls by e-mail and on the Web. A few years ago, the company put in a high-bandwidth telephone line. But even then, Mr. Quinn said, the stream of data will probably fill those lines until bigger ones come along. So, he said, "Instead of just buying more bandwidth, we decided to address the problem." This week, a month after installing the software, Ritvik planned to put into practice a new policy requiring employees to use good judgement in their use of the network. It will also warn them that their e-mail messages may be monitored.

Revealing that employees are being monitored is a good business practice, according to the American Management Association. At some point, it may be required by law in much of the United States. Mr. Quinn is hoping that monitoring will be a powerful deterrent and convince employees not to waste company time and bandwidth. From what he has seen, at least 50 percent of the company's e-mail is not related to work. And, he says, certain names keep appearing on lists of heavy e-mail users, including an employee he has nicknamed the herbal-remedy guy, who has spent hours looking at the Web site of Deepak Chopra, the author of spiritual books, and sending messages about herbal therapies.

Others send jokes. "Look at this guy," he said, as he pointed to a subject heading titled, "Joke of the Day" and another titled "Women Drivers." He scrolled further, displaying even more jokes all sent by the same employee. "That's all he's been doing for the last hour," Mr. Quinn said, throwing up his hands in irritation. It is not his responsibility to monitor employee productivity, he said, but he cannot help but wonder how such people get their work done.

Ritvik employees had mixed emotions about the policy. "It is an invasion of your privacy, I guess," said Karen Trainor, the company's North American distribution supervisor. "If someone knows everything you are writing, that's not really fair." But, she added, she had heard that the company was trying to strengthen its networks and might need to check e-mail traffic to do so. Besides, she has known Mr. Quinn for years and

continued

---

5. *seek:* to try to do something
6. *peeking:* secretly looking
7. *jeopardize:* to put in danger; to threaten

trusts him. "If that's what they are doing, I guess they have a reason to do
75 it," she said.

Once monitoring becomes routine, it also falls into grayer areas[8] of the
law, according to some lawyers familiar with workplace privacy issues.
A few lawyers have argued that a casual e-mail exchange is more like a
telephone conversation than a printed memo and should be protected in
80 the same way that wiretap[9] laws generally prohibit government agencies
and some businesses from secretly listening to personal conversations.

"Would you entrust the government with this kind of information?" asked
Jeremy E. Gruber, legal director for the National Workrights Institute at a
recent New York Bar Association[10] discussion on electronic privacy. "Why
85 do we think that employers will use it in a wonderful way?"

Mr. Quinn acknowledges that monitoring systems can be abused. For
example, he has no trouble imagining a network manager who takes
offense at an e-mail message most people would consider harmless—
and who makes life difficult for the sender as a result. "You have to ask:
90 whose opinion draws the line?"[11] Mr. Quinn said.

---

8. *gray areas:* areas that are not clearly right or wrong
9. *wiretap:* a device on a telephone that allows others to listen to the
   conversation secretly
10. *New York Bar Association:* an organization for attorneys
11. *draw the line:* decide when to stop an action

A. General Understanding

1. Understanding the Reading

*Answer these questions in your own words. Then share your answers with
a partner.*

1. What's this article about?

2. How do the people in the article feel about monitoring employee e-mail?

Mr. Quinn, systems manager:	
Jeremy E. Gruber, legal director:	
Karen Trainor, Ritvik supervisor:	

3. What does the American Management Association recommend to
   employers who monitor office e-mail? How do you feel about this?

2. Why Do Companies Monitor Office E-mail?

Look at this list of the things that companies look for in employee e-mail messages. Then, using information from the article, match what companies monitor with the best or most appropriate reason for the monitoring.

What companies monitor in e-mail

Reasons

__b__ 1. Words like "confidential"

a. Off-color jokes or ethnic jokes can be reasons for lawsuits

_____ 2. Subject lines with **Fwd** (forward) or **Re** (about) appearing several times in one message

b. Company secrets may be revealed, deliberately or not

_____ 3. Numerous messages sent in one day by a single employee to people outside

c. They overload networks, slow computers, and may crash the system

_____ 4. Headlines with phrases like "Job Hunt" or "resume"

d. They suggest the sender is goofing off instead of working

_____ 5. Messages with attachments over a megabyte in size

e. These are likely to be forwarded jokes or back-and-forth messages

_____ 6. Racial insults or words like "sex" and "babe"

f. These indicate an employee is getting ready to leave the company

3. What Do You Think?

Discuss these questions in a small group. Give at least one reason for your opinions.

1. Is casual e-mail similar to a telephone conversation or a printed memo? The U.S. Constitution says that government and the police are not allowed to secretly listen to your personal telephone conversations unless they can convince a judge that they have evidence of criminal activity. Should e-mail also be protected in this way?

2. Should citizens have the same sort of protection at work as they have in their own homes? Why or why not?

B. Working with Language

1. Vocabulary in Context

Read these excerpts from a chat room discussion of workplace privacy. Then choose the word or phrase with a similar meaning to replace the word or phrase in bold.

Jerry, a waiter

I'm ready to quit. I'm being videotaped in the bathroom!! My boss **installed** _C_ some video **surveillance** ___ equipment in the restroom because he wants to be sure that the employees wash their hands before leaving. He's worried that some customer might sue him if they don't. This certainly feels like an **invasion** ___ of my privacy. If the restroom isn't private, what is?

---

a. violation
b. supervision
c. put in

Jane, an office supervisor

My employees used to spend hours playing video games and sending jokes to friends. I tried sending memos, but they just closed their office doors. So I bought equipment that **enables** ___ me to **monitor** ___ what they are doing whenever they are online. I had **mixed emotions** ___ about **snooping on** ___ them, but how else was I supposed to **dissuade them from** ___ wasting company time when they refused to listen to me?

---

a. persuade them against
b. makes it possible for
c. confused feelings
d. observe on a regular basis
e. secretly watching

Anna, a systems manager

I need advice!!! I work with my company's e-mail system. My boss asked me to be **on the lookout for** ___ key words in e-mails like "sex" or "job listing." I agreed, but I didn't realize what this would really mean. For example, I found out that the office manager and his assistant write secret love letters to each other on a **routine** ___ basis. Because of recent lawsuits accusing superiors of **sexual harassment** ___, our company policy **prohibits** ___ office dating. So, if I tell about the love letters, both of them could be fired. If I don't, I **jeopardize** ___ my own position. What should I do?

a. regular
b. searching for
c. risk losing
d. forbids
e. mistreatment of or discrimination
   against a person because of gender

2. Discuss the Situations

Discuss the situations in the above exercise in small groups. Then summarize your group's discussion in your notebook.

1. How do you feel about the restaurant owner's decision to use surveillance equipment in the restroom? Why is the owner doing this?

2. How would you feel if you were one of Jane's employees? How else can Jane monitor her employees' behavior? *give them time line, firewall*

3. How do you feel about Anna's situation? Should businesses ask employees to monitor each other and report abuses? Should employees be prohibited from dating each other?

III **Prewriting Activities**

A. Summarizing and Responding to Academic Research

The following excerpts have been adapted from an article entitled "Technology, Workplace Privacy and Personhood" written by William S. Brown for the *Journal of Business Ethics*.

Read the excerpts. Then complete the exercises that follow each excerpt.

Excerpt 1: A Historical Perspective

George Orwell, in his classic negative utopian novel *1984*, has described what many believe to be the ultimate in privacy-shattering totalitarianism, the land of Oceania. In Oceania ". . . there was of course no way of knowing whether you were being watched at any given moment . . . . It was even conceivable that they watched everybody all the time . . . . You had to live—did live, from habit that became instinct, in the assumption that every sound you made was overheard, and, except in darkness, every movement scrutinized" (Orwell 6-7). When written, Orwell's novel offered a foreboding look at future society. We have now advanced technologically to the point, where if desired, this kind of surveillance is easily possible. In many workplaces it is already a reality.

With a partner, answer the following questions. Then use your answers to write your own summary and response to Excerpt 1 in your notebook.

1. How much privacy do people have in Oceania?

2. What does Orwell's vision of the future remind Brown of in the present?

3. What do you think of this comparison?

Excerpt 2: A Psychological Perspective

How do workers respond to a panoptic, or all-seeing, society? Erich Fromm (41) feels that modern industrial society forces people to be passive. This passivity[1] is just one symptom of what he calls the "syndrome of alienation"[2] that is characteristic of our society. Other symptoms include feelings of powerlessness, loneliness, and free-floating anxiety. Fromm connects these feelings to submission[3] to a perceived total control by some authoritarian figure or institution.

Some psychologists feel workers experience shame[4] due to the new visibility of the high-tech workplace. One way to cope with the dilemma of total visibility and fear of shame is through conformity.[5] According to Zuboff, workers accept the fact that they are being watched and adapt their behavior to conform to the rules and regulations of the company. Unfortunately, such workers experience a loss of autonomy[6] which may lead to depression, and nervous breakdown.

---

1. *passivity:* a lack of energy or will
2. *alienation:* a sense of being separate or alone
3. *submission:* an act of giving in to the control of another
4. *shame:* a painful emotion caused by a sense of guilt
5. *conformity:* the act of adapting oneself to the standards of those in authority
6. *autonomy:* the quality or state of being self-governing; free will

With a partner, answer the following questions. Then use your answers to write your own summary and response to Excerpt 2 in your notebook.

1. What are the symptoms of Fromm's "syndrome of alienation"? What does Fromm connect these feelings to?

2. Brown states that Zuboff claims workers experience "shame" at constant monitoring. How do they cope with this shame?

3. What might a loss of autonomy lead to?

4. Do you agree with this analysis of the results of working in a panoptic environment?

Excerpt 3: A Business Perspective

Albert Bandura links a lack of workplace privacy to low motivation, poor performance, difficulty with goal-setting, and poor reactions to supervisory feedback. If care is not taken in the high-tech workplace, technology will divide the individual from his authentic self, and thereby destroy his sense of being and damage his performance. Thus, a constant scanning of worker attitudes towards reduced privacy is essential to maintaining workplace harmony, as indicated in Figure 1.

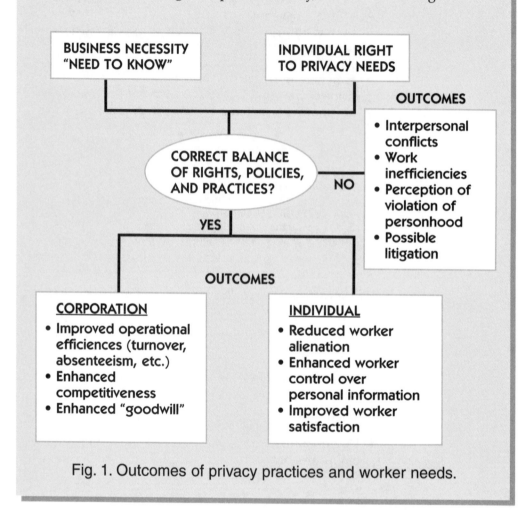

Fig. 1. Outcomes of privacy practices and worker needs.

With a partner, answer the following questions. Then use your answers to write your own summary and response to Excerpt 3 in your notebook.

1. How does a lack of workplace privacy affect workers? What is the result?

2. What should employers do to help build a harmonious workplace? What does Figure 1 illustrate?

3. What do you think about the system proposed by Bandura?

B. Open for Discussion

Discuss these questions in a small group. Then choose one topic and summarize your opinion of it and the opinion of someone who disagrees with you in your notebook.

1. How do you respond to authority? Do you work better when you are supervised or when you are left to work on your own? How do most people work best?

2. Airlines frequently test employees for the presence of drugs. Unfortunately, the tests often give false positive results. If an employee has used ibuprophen, a pain reliever sold without a prescription, he or she might test positive for marijuana, an illegal substance. Should employers have the right to do drug testing?

3. What does the following quote mean? Do you agree or disagree with it? How does it relate to workplace monitoring?

   Power tends to corrupt, and absolute power corrupts absolutely.
   Lord Acton, 1887

4. Under the Americans with Disabilities Act, U.S. employers cannot deny employment to an applicant with a specific illness. However, the employer can do genetic screening of potential employees and deny him or her employment if the candidate has a biological predisposition for a number of illnesses. Thus a candidate can be denied a position because he may someday contract the illness, but *not if he already has the illness*. Should an employer be allowed to do genetic screening of job candidates?

IV Structured Writing Focus

 YOUR TASK

Write a five-paragraph essay about the advantages and disadvantages of workplace monitoring of employees by employers. Indicate whether you are in favor of it. Use information from the readings in this unit and information from your own experience as support for your opinions.

ALTERNATIVE TASK: Write a three- to five-paragraph essay in which you explain the following quote. Indicate whether you agree or disagree with it and use detailed examples to support your opinion. Use examples from history, current events, and/or personal experience.

Power may be compared to a great river; while kept within its bounds it is both beautiful and useful, but when it overflows its banks, it is then too impetuous to be stemmed; it bears down all before it, and brings destruction and desolation wherever it comes.

Andrew Hamilton (1676–1741)

A. Starting to Write

Brainstorming

FOR THE MAIN TASK

Use this chart to help you start organizing your thoughts. Write down anything you can think of, even though you might not use it in your essay. Use your own words.

Advantages	
Disadvantages	
My opinion	

Write notes for your essay in your notebook on these questions.

1. What facts, statistics, or quotes do you have to support your opinions?

2. Is there any information in the unit readings that supports your position?

3. What are the sources of your support?

Write notes for your essay in your notebook on these questions.

For the introduction . . .

1. Look at the quote. Circle the noun phrases in the quote. Which ones are the most important?

2. How do the ideas in the quote relate to each other?

3. What are the key words in the quote?

4. What does the quote mean?

5. Do you agree or disagree with the quote? How will you support your opinion?

For the body paragraphs . . .

1. What examples from history can you think of to support your opinion?

2. What examples from current events can you cite to support your opinion?

3. What examples from your own life and experience can you cite?

4. Is there any information in the unit readings that supports your position?

5. What are the sources of your support?

For the conclusion . . .

1. How can you restate your thesis without repeating it?

2. What key words from the quote and your introduction can you use to unify your essay?

Use this chart to help you start organizing your thoughts. Write down anything you can think of, even though you might not use it in your essay. Use your own words.

Body ¶1	
Body ¶2	
Body ¶3	

B. Preparing the First Draft

1. Using a Summary as the Introduction to an Essay

As discussed in previous units, many essays are based on readings. One way to respond to a reading is to include a summary of it in the introduction to your essay. Then you can respond to the reading in the body paragraphs of your essay and/or add more support from other sources: articles, graphs, or charts.

Read this sample introduction for an essay on the topic of the advantages of workplace monitoring. Then do the exercises that follow.

"It was a bright cold day in April, and the clocks were striking thirteen." From the opening sentence in his novel 1984, George Orwell creates a feeling of unease. There is obviously something very wrong with the society he describes. By comparing today's workplace to Orwell's Oceana "the ultimate in privacy-shattering totalitarianism," William S. Brown paints a frightening, but unrealistic, picture of employer–employee relations in his Journal of Business Ethics article, "Technology, Workplace Privacy and Personhood." Today's workplace has indeed changed as a result of workplace monitoring, but it is not the "foreboding" landscape described in 1984—far from it. The advantages of workplace monitoring in today's business climate far outweigh the disadvantages.

1. Underline and label the hook. What makes this hook interesting?

2. What important information is included in sentence 4?

3. Underline and label the thesis statement. Is it a direct or indirect thesis?

4. How would you organize the body of this essay based on the introduction?

5. Which key words would you use in your conclusion?

2. Using the Conclusion to Unify Your Essay

Like most essays, the conclusion for an advantages/disadvantages essay generally begins with a restatement of your thesis. This should rephrase, not repeat, the thesis. Other features of a good conclusion include

- key words from the thesis to unify the essay

- a summary of the main points from the body of the essay

- suggestions, advice, or a warning to readers about the consequences of not following the advice

- something to think about after the reader has finished the essay

Read this sample conclusion for the same essay. Then do the exercises that follow.

Technology has changed for the better the way we work today. Employees recognize the need for monitoring and do not equate it with Orwell's "Big Brother" totalitarian society. Employers can now monitor employees to be sure they are not wasting company time and money. The workplace is safer because of drug testing and video-taping. In fact, without workplace monitoring, the workplace would function less efficiently and be a far more dangerous environment. If you owned a company, wouldn't you want your employees to be carefully supervised?

1. Underline and label the restatement of the thesis. Which key words are used? What kinds of things did the author do to rephrase the thesis?

2. Does the author offer any advice? Any warnings? Something to think about?

3. Which key phrases sum up topics in the body of the essay?

4. How does this conclusion help unify this essay?

NOTE TO WRITERS:
To avoid plagiarism, put all material in your own words in your essay. If you want to use someone else's exact words, you must add quotation marks around the quote and cite the source. (See Section D of this unit for instruction.)

3. Organizing Your Essay

Study this block diagram of a five-paragraph advantages/disadvantages essay to plan a first draft of your essay. In your notebook, draw your own diagram and write your notes in each of its sections.

MAIN TASK	ALTERNATIVE TASK

INTRODUCTION
Hook
Summary or general statements
Thesis statement

INTRODUCTION
Hook (optional)
Explanation and analysis of quote
Thesis statement

BODY ¶ 1
Advantages of workplace monitoring
Topic sentence
Summary of research as support

BODY ¶ 1
Support for your opinion
Topic sentence
Examples from history / current events / personal experience

Transitional sentence

Transitional sentence

BODY ¶ 2
Disadvantages of workplace monitoring
Topic sentence
Summary of research as support

BODY ¶ 2
Support for your opinion
Topic sentence
Examples from history / current events / personal experience

Transitional sentence

Transitional sentence

BODY ¶ 3
Your opinion on workplace monitoring
Topic sentence
Summary of research as support
Concluding sentence

BODY ¶ 3
Support for your opinion
Topic sentence
Examples from history / current events / personal experience
Concluding sentence

CONCLUSION
Restatement of thesis
Summary of main points
Advice and / or warning

CONCLUSION
Restatement of thesis
Summary of main points
Reference to quote
Advice and/or warning

*Write a **first draft** of your essay. Remember to write in complete sentences and try to use some of the vocabulary and structures that you have practiced in this unit.*

C. Revising the First Draft

When you have finished writing your first draft, read it to a partner.

CHECKLIST FOR REVISING THE FIRST DRAFT

When you listen to your partner's essay and when you discuss your own, keep these questions in mind:

1. Is the author's opinion on the subject clear?

2. For the alternative task: Is the quote analyzed well in the introduction? Is the author's opinion of the quote clear?

3. Is information from the academic research and readings summarized well? Is it used to support opinions?

4. Are any quotes from the readings used? If so, are they properly presented?

5. Does the conclusion refer back to key ideas in the introduction?

6. Does the author leave the reader with something to think about?

After discussing your essay with a partner, you may want to go add, change, or omit some information.

*Now write a **second draft** that includes all of your additions and changes.*

D. Editing the Second Draft

1. The "Works Cited" List

Academic books and articles usually have a full list of all source material at the end. When quoting information from an outside source, you should also include a Works Cited list, or bibliography, at the end of your essay.

Most authors use the Modern Language Association (MLA) Style. The Works Cited list should be arranged alphabetically by author's last name and should not be numbered. Here are some examples of properly cited sources. Notice that punctuation is very important.*

BOOK

Author. Book Title. Publication City: Publisher, Year of publication.

Orwell, George. 1984. New York: Harcourt Brace & Co., 1949.

NEWSPAPER ARTICLE

Author. "Article title." Newspaper title Day Month Year, edition: Page(s).

Singletary, Michelle. "E-Mail Humor: Punch Lines Can Carry Price." Washington Post 18 Mar. 1997, final edition: A1.

MAGAZINE ARTICLE

Author. "Article Title." Magazine Title (Day) Month Year: Page(s)

Cooper, Simon. "Who's Spying on You?" Popular Mechanics Jan. 2005: 56+.

Note: If pages are continuous, indicate beginning and end pages (56–60). If not, list the beginning page and a plus sign (56+).

SCHOLARLY JOURNAL

Author. "Article title." Journal title Volume number (Year): Page(s).

Leap, Thomas. "When You Can Fire for Off-Duty Conduct." Harvard Business Review 30 (1988): 78–101.

Answer these questions with your classmates. Refer to the Works Cited list in the box above.

1. Which types of titles require quotation marks?

2. Which type of title should appear underlined (or italic)?

3. How do you write the author's name?

---

*According to MLA style, italics and underlining can be used interchangeably. Throughout this book, we have used underlining. Ask your instructor which method he or she prefers.

Look at this partial Works Cited list for the William S. Brown article* on pages 74–76. Rewrite the sources correctly. Then arrange them alphabetically. Share your answers with the class.

Journal of Business Ethics 1996, William S. Brown, "Technology, workplace privacy and personhood." Volume15, pages 1237-39, 1250-53.

Social Learning Theory by A. Bandura, published by Prentice Hall in Englewood Cliffs, NJ in 1977.

Erich Fromm: Escape from Freedom (Avon Books, NY) 1968

"Abuse of Sick Leave Rises and Companies Fight Back", New York Times (Nov. 30): A12. P.T. Kilborn 1992

Simon, H.A.: 1977, "What Computers Mean for Man and Society," Science March 18, pages 86-91.

Brave New Workplace (Viking Books, NY), 1985, Howard, R.

Foucault, M. (Vintage Books) New York, 1979 Discipline and Punish: The Birth of Prison

1988, S. Zuboff, Basic Books: NY, "In the Age of the Smart Machine: The Future of Work and Power."

_____

_____

_____

_____

_____

_____

_____

_____

_____

*Note: Whenever possible, use the full name of the author as it appears on the title page of the book. Brown does not use the MLA system. He uses the APA system, which requires the first initial only.

2. Online References

Additional information is needed for online references to help the reader locate the source accurately. Indicate both the date when the article was published AND the date you visited the site. Also include the URL in angle brackets. See the MLA guide for more information.

ARTICLE FROM A WEBSITE

Author. "Title of article." Title of publication or website. Date of publication. Date of visit to the website <URL>.

Gibson, Dena. "Employee Monitoring: Is There Privacy in the Workplace?" Privacy Rights Clearinghouse. Mar. 1993. 12 Jan. 2005 <http://www.privacyrights.org/fs/fs7-work.htm>.

ONLINE ENCYCLOPEDIA

"subject." Title of publication. Date of publication. Title of website Date of visit to the website <URL>.

"genetic disease, human." Encyclopaedia Britannica. 2005. Encyclopaedia Britannica Online 20 Jan. 2005 <http://search.eb.com/ed/article?tocId=50766>.

Go online and do research on the topic of "Workplace Privacy." List at least three online references. You may want to add some information from these sources to your second draft. Be sure to use the correct format in your Works Cited list.

_____

_____

_____

_____

_____

_____

_____

_____

_____

_____

3. Citations within the Text

When quoting information from someone else, you need to refer the reader to the correct source in your Works Cited list.

Cite the author's name and the page number within the source

"It was a bright cold day in April, and the clocks were striking thirteen" (Orwell 1).

This tells the reader that this quote can be found on page 1 of the Orwell entry in the Works Cited list at the end of the essay.

Use the author's name in your text and cite only the page number

You can also use the author's name in the sentence and indicate only the page number of the source material in parentheses. This is the preferred method for online citations:

Orwell begins his novel <u>1984</u> with an unsettling line, "It was a bright cold day in April, and the clocks were striking thirteen" (1).

Look over the second draft of your essay. Have you included support from the readings in this unit? If not, try to add some quotes from the reading on pages 68–70 or the excerpts on pages 74–76. Be sure to cite your sources correctly in a Works Cited list and inside the text of your essay (use the page numbers from this book in your citation).

E. Preparing the Final Draft

Reread your second draft and correct any errors you find. Put a check (✓) in each space as you edit for these points. Then write your corrected final version.

CHECKLIST FOR EDITING THE SECOND DRAFT

_____ **citations within the text of the essay**

_____ **the use of quotation marks and underlining in titles**

_____ **the "Works Cited" list**

Additional Writing Opportunities

Write about one of the following topics.

1. Some workplaces have a policy that prohibits employees from dating. Write an essay in which you discuss the advantages and disadvantages of such a policy. You can do research on the topic or use your personal opinions and experience to support your points.

2. Write an essay that analyzes the following quote. Explain what the quote means and whether you agree or disagree with it. Use examples from history, current events, and/or personal experience to support your opinions.

> *Far better to conceive of power as consisting in part of the knowledge of when not to use all the power you have. Far better to be one who knows that if you reserve the power not to use all your power, you will lead others far more successfully and well.*

> A. Bartlett Giacometti (1938–1989)
> President of Yale University

3. Write an essay about a time in your life when you felt powerless in a difficult situation. Use detailed descriptions to make your writing more interesting. Try to appeal to as many senses as possible in your descriptions.

4. Do research on a related topic such as genetic screening of job applicants or sexual harassment in the workplace. Use a variety of sources, such as statistics, newspapers, scholarly journals, books, and online sources. Write an essay summarizing your research and giving your opinion about the questions raised by your research. Include a Works Cited list at the end of your essay and cite your sources throughout.

MIRROR, MIRROR, ON THE WALL

Beauty Quiz

	True	False
1. Attractive students receive better grades in school than unattractive students.		
2. When attractive and unattractive people are in a relationship, it is usually the unattractive one who makes most of the decisions.		
3. Prisoners with physical defects who received cosmetic surgery were less likely to be repeat offenders.		
4. Attractive children get higher grades on standardized achievement tests.		
5. If a man is with a pretty woman, people, in general, think the man isn't very intelligent.		
6. Less attractive people usually beat out more attractive people for secretarial jobs because interviewers assume the less attractive people are more competent.		
7. Total strangers assume more attractive people are less honest and interesting than less attractive people.		
8. Men who are at least six feet tall make more money and are promoted faster than shorter men are.		

WRITING A CAUSE-AND-EFFECT ESSAY

In this unit you will practice:
- developing different types of support
- writing up research studies
- showing cause and effect
- outlining an essay

Editing focus:
- adverbial clauses
- causal connectors
- reported speech

I Fluency Practice: Freewriting

Take the quiz above. Guess the answers by putting a check (✓) in the column under True or False. Then choose one or two questions from the Beauty Quiz and write your comments. Share your thoughts with others in a small group.

89

II ▸ **Reading for Writing**

This excerpt from "The Face of Beauty" by Diane Ackerman discusses the reality behind the old saying, "beauty is only skin deep."

THE FACE OF BEAUTY
by Diane Ackerman

We may pretend that beauty is only skin deep, but Aristotle[1] was right when he observed "beauty is a far greater recommendation than any letter of introduction."

The sad truth is that attractive people do better in school, where they
5 receive more help, better grades, and less punishment; at work, where they are rewarded with higher pay, more prestigious[2] jobs, and faster promotions and make most of the decisions; and among total strangers, who assume
10 them to be interesting, honest, virtuous, and successful.

In fairy tales, the first stories most of us hear, the
15 heroes are handsome, the heroines are beautiful, and the wicked are ugly. Children learn implicitly[3] that good people are beautiful and bad
20 people are ugly, and society restates that message in many subtle ways as they grow older. So perhaps it's not surprising that handsome cadets at West Point[4] achieve a higher rank by the time they graduate, or that a judge is more likely to give an attractive criminal a
25 shorter sentence.

In a 1968 study conducted in the New York City prison system, men with scars, deformities,[5] and other physical defects were divided into three groups. The first group received cosmetic surgery, the second intensive counseling and therapy, and the third no treatment at all. A year after their release from
30 prison, when the researchers checked to see how the men were doing, they discovered that those who had received cosmetic surgery had adjusted the best and were less likely to return to prison.

1. *Aristotle:* ancient Greek philosopher (384-322 B.C.E.)
2. *prestigious:* bringing admiration or respect for someone because it is a sign of wealth or success
3. *implicit:* indirect
4. *West Point:* a military academy in New York state
5. *deformities:* bodily malformations

In experiments conducted by corporations, when different photos were attached to the same resume, the more attractive person was hired.

35 Prettier babies are treated better than homelier[6] ones, not just by strangers but by the baby's parents as well. Mothers snuggle,[7] kiss, talk to, play more with their baby if it's cute; and fathers of cute babies are also more involved with them.

Attractive children get higher grades on their achievement tests,
40 probably because their good looks win praise, attention, and encouragement from adults. In a 1975 study, teachers were asked to evaluate the records of an eight-year-old who had a low IQ and poor grades. Every teacher saw the same records, but the photo of a pretty child was attached to some, and
45 to others that of a homely child. The teachers were more likely to recommend that the homely child be sent to a class for slow learners.

The beauty of another can be a
50 valuable accessory.[8] One particularly interesting study asked people to look at a photo of a man and a woman, and to evaluate only the man. As it turns out, if the woman on the man's
55 arm was pretty, the man was thought to be more intelligent and successful than if the woman was unattractive.

Shocking as the results of these and similar experiments might be,
60 they confirm what we've known for ages: Like it or not, a woman's face has always been to some extent a commodity.[9] Historically, a beautiful woman was often able to marry her way out of a lower class and poverty. We remember legendary beauties like Cleopatra and Helen of Troy as symbols of how beauty can be powerful enough to cause the downfall of
65 great leaders and change the course of empires.

For men, beauty can also be a powerful asset, but the real commodity is height. One study followed the professional lives of 17,000 men. Those who were at least six feet tall did much better, received more money, were promoted faster, and rose to more prestigious positions. Perhaps tall men
70 trigger[10] childhood memories of looking up to authority—only our parents and other adults were tall, and they had all the power to punish or protect, to give absolute love, set our wishes in motion, or block our hopes.

---

6. *homely:* plain, not good-looking
7. *snuggle:* cuddle
8. *accessory:* something that goes with something else
9. *commodity:* a thing of use or advantage
10. *trigger:* activate

A. General Understanding

1. Understanding the Main Idea

In your notebook, write the main idea of this essay in your own words. Compare your answer with a partner.

2. Identifying Support

Go back to the Beauty Quiz on page 89 and use your understanding of the reading to correct your answers. Discuss the corrections with a partner. Did any answer surprise you?

3. Writing Up Research Studies

Research studies are often used to support the main idea of an essay. Write up the studies cited in The Face of Beauty *on pages 90–91 by filling in the missing information.*

	Prison Study
1. Participants	Prisoners with scars, deformities, and other physical defects
2. Aim of study	To see how the physical appearance of prisoners affects their ability to adjust to life after their release from prison.
3. Procedure	Participants were divided into three groups. Group A got cosmetic surgery, Group B got intensive counseling and psychological therapy, and Group C was the control group: they received no treatment.
4. Results (one year later)	
5. Explanation	

	Business Study
1. Participants	
2. Aim of study	
3. Procedure	
4. Results	
5. Explanation	

	Education Study
1. Participants	
2. Aim of study	
3. Procedure	
4. Results	
5. Explanation	

B. Working with Language

1. Understanding Euphemisms

Euphemisms give people a more polite way of saying something that might be embarrassing or unpleasant. Because they are not precise, however, they can often distort or hide the truth. Not all euphemisms are appropriate in all situations.

Each of the columns in the chart below is headed by an adjective that most people avoid using in polite society. Read the euphemistic words and phrases and put each into the appropriate category in the chart. Add any other euphemisms you can think of. Then put a check (✓) next to the words that would be appropriate to use when describing your boss or teacher.

big-boned	husky	plump
compact	mature	senior
diminutive	not terribly attractive	slight of build
dowdy	of a certain age	stout
full-figured	past his/her prime	unremarkable
homely	plain	veteran

Fat	Old	Ugly	Short
	past his prime mature ✓		

2. Using Euphemisms

Rewrite these personal ads to make the people sound more appealing. Use euphemisms from Exercise 1 and your own ideas.

I am a short, heavy woman, who is not young. I'm also far from beautiful. I am, however, a friendly, outgoing person. In addition, I have a good sense of humor. I'm looking for an older person who is interested in the arts, travel, and films.

_____

_____

_____

_____

_____

_____

I am old man with a thick, short body. Although I'm rather ugly, I'm light on my feet. I've been told I'm an excellent dancer. I like to take long walks, visit museums, and go to the theatre. As I'm very well read, I'm an excellent conversationalist.

_____

_____

_____

_____

_____

_____

3. The Language of Cause-and-Effect

Read the chart and notice the punctuation in each structure.

CAUSE	TRANSITION	EFFECT
Unattractive people don't receive as much help in school as attractive people;	**as a result, consequently, because of this,**	they receive lower grades.
Employers assume attractive people are more competent than unattractive people.	**This is the reason for This is responsible for This leads/contributes to This results in**	unattractive people being unable to compete in the job market.

EFFECT	TRANSITION	CAUSE
Many unattractive people are unable to compete in the job market with attractive people	**because because of the fact that since**	employers consistently choose to promote attractive people over unattractive ones.
The inability of unattractive people to compete in the job market with attractive people	**results from is due to is a result of is a consequence of**	discrimination by employers.

TRANSITION	CAUSE	EFFECT
Since Because	unattractive people are presented as bad or evil in fairy tales,	children learn that heroes are handsome and bad people are ugly.

	CAUSE	EFFECT
(so . . . that)	Unattractive people experience **so** much discrimination	**that** they develop low self-esteem.
(such . . . that)	Discrimination is **such** a common experience for unattractive people	**that** they come to believe they deserve it.

4. Building Cause-and-Effect Sentences

Refer to the chart on page 96. Complete each idea and use one of the cause / effect expressions given.

1. (is the reason for/is responsible for/leads to/contributes to/results in)
   Early on in life, people learn implicitly that good people are beautiful or handsome and bad people are ugly. This message is reinforced in a variety of ways by society. This deeply held belief about attractive and unattractive people . . .

   leads to handsome cadets achieving a higher rank by the

   time they graduate.

2. (is the reason for/is responsible for/leads to/contributes to/results in)
   People assume attractive people are more interesting, virtuous, honest, and successful than unattractive people. This assumption . . .

   _____

   _____

3. (as a result/consequently/because of this)
   Unattractive people are considered less competent and creative than unattractive people; . . .

   _____

   _____

4. (so...that)
   Unattractive people experience **so** much discrimination in life . . .

   _____

   _____

5. (Because/since)

   _____ their good looks win praise, attention, and

   encouragement from adults, . . .

   _____

   _____

III Prewriting Activities

A. Identifying Cause and Effect

In this *New York Times* article, Sandra Blakeslee reports on some of the causes and effects of negative body image. Here is the beginning of the article.

HOW YOU SEE YOURSELF: POTENTIAL FOR BIG PROBLEMS

by Sandra Blakeslee

An overweight girl is teased for being fat. A boy with protruding ears is called "Dumbo." An adolescent girl is ashamed of her flat chest. A teenage boy is taunted for his underdeveloped muscles.

5   Most people who are teased for looking "different" in childhood and adolescence manage to ignore it. But many young people cannot, new research shows. Negative body images take root in their minds and even years later they see themselves as their tormenters did in childhood.

"We always knew body image could influence behavior," said Dr. Thomas F. Cash, a professor of psychology at Old Dominion University in
10 Norfolk, Va., and a leading expert on body images. "But it is surprising to see how lasting the images can be."

By studying body images that endure, he said, researchers are gaining insights into personality development, eating disorders, motives for plastic surgery and the cultural standards of physical attractiveness for American
15 men and women.

Read the pairs of sentences based on information from the remainder of the Blakeslee article. Label the cause sentence and the effect sentence. Then combine the two sentences into one sentence using a transition from the chart on page 96.

1. __cause__ a. Some children are teased a lot in school.

   __effect__ b. They develop signs of depression that can extend into adulthood.

Because some children are teased a lot in school, they develop signs of depression that can extend into adulthood.

2. _____ a. People often decide to undergo cosmetic surgery.

   _____ b. People feel self-conscious about the way they look.

3. _____ a. Psychologist Thomas F. Cash found that young children quickly absorb definitions of attractiveness.

   _____ b. When children do not conform to these standards, they may be teased.

4. _____ a. As they grow up, these children develop a great loss of self-esteem.

_____ b. As grown-ups, they develop deep depression.

5. _____ a. People who were teased a lot as children about their weight develop a negative body image.

_____ b. People develop eating disorders.

6. _____ a. Children become intensely self-conscious about their defect.

_____ b. Children are teased or criticized by parents, older siblings, teachers, coaches or other significant people in their lives.

7. _____ a. People are turning to psychological therapy.

_____ b. People want to get help identifying and changing unrealistic thinking patterns

B. Point of View Writing

Choose ONE topic to write about. Share your writing with a partner.

1. When you were a child, you were a little overweight. One day at school, you were teased and called "fat" by some of your classmates. If you could go back in time, what would you say to the children who teased you? What would you do about their behavior or yours?

2. You suspect that your teenaged daughter (or sister) has the beginnings of an eating disorder. You know there is a lot of pressure at her high school to be very thin. How would you deal with this situation?

C. Open for Discussion

Discuss these questions in a small group.

1. Is there a universal idea of beauty? What does a physically attractive woman look like? What does a handsome man look like?

2. How do Hollywood movies, advertisements, and the fashion industry contribute to what we think is beautiful? Are these realistic ideas? Why or why not?

3. What remedies are there in our society for people who are considered or who consider themselves unattractive?

4. What do you think could be done to change the way prospective employers and others in society treat people who are not very attractive?

After your discussion, choose one question and write about it. Share your writing with the group.

IV Structured Writing Focus

YOUR TASK

Write a five-paragraph essay in which you discuss the causes and effects of discrimination based on the way people look, and the effects of this discrimination on the individual and on society as a whole.

ALTERNATIVE TASK: **Write a five-paragraph essay about the causes and effects of discrimination against handicapped people, women, or older people.**

A. Starting to Write

Brainstorming

FOR THE MAIN TASK

In your notebook, write your thoughts on these questions.

1. What messages do children receive about their appearance?

2. How are these messages communicated to them?

*What are some **causes** of negative body images? Check off some contributing factors you want to write about. Add any others you can think of.*

_____ pressure from family

_____ pressure from friends or classmates

_____ competition or bullying

_____ advertisements and the media

_____ the entertainment industry

*Check off some **effects** of this discrimination that you would like to write about. Add any others you can think of.*

For the individual:

_____ depression

_____ lack of self-confidence

_____ eating disorders

_____ loss of ambition and the drive to succeed

_____ the perceived need for cosmetic surgery or procedures

For society:

_____ society loses the contributions of many people

_____ some people are angry and feel resentful

Other factors:

_____

_____

_____

What can be done about these causes and effects?

FOR THE ALTERNATIVE TASK

In your notebook, write your thoughts on these questions.

1. When you were a child, what messages did you receive about children who were physically or mentally disabled?

2. What messages did you receive about the appropriate behavior for boys? Appropriate behavior for girls?

3. What is the effect of this type of discrimination on individuals?

4. What effects do they have on society?

5. Has society attempted to deal with the causes and/or effects of this type of prejudice against certain people? How?

B. Preparing the First Draft

1. "SAFER"

Use several different types of support in your essay. Try to use at least one piece of support from each of the "SAFER" categories: **S**tatistics, **A**necdotes, **F**acts, **E**xamples, **R**easons.

Look back at the article on pages 90–91. Find at least one example of each type of support and write it below. Compare your results with a partner.

Statistics: _____

Anecdotes: _____

Facts: _____

Examples: _____

Reasons: _____

2. Outlining a Cause-and-Effect Essay

INTRODUCTORY PARAGRAPH

The introductory paragraph of a cause-and-effect essay should take one of two approaches:

- **Demonstrate that a problem exists**
  or
- **State a commonly held belief that you will disprove in your essay** (such as, "beauty is only skin deep").

Use anecdotes, examples, statistics, or facts in your introduction. As in other types of essays, end your introduction with a **thesis statement** that highlights what you intend to discuss in your essay.

Help this student create a general outline for a cause and effect essay on discrimination against women. Start with the introduction. What support could the writer include?

Introduction

Approach: Problem: far fewer women than men in high positions in U.S. companies and government posts.

Support: _____

_____

_____

_____

_____

Thesis: Because there is a bias toward men in the business world and in politics, women and their interests are underrepresented in the marketplace and in society.

Paragraphs 2, 3, and 4 can be organized in several different ways:

causes		causes		cause/effect
causes	or	effects	or	cause/effect
effects		effects		cause/effect

Start each paragraph with a topic sentence stating the nature of the paragraph. Use all types of support in the body paragraphs—SAFER.

This student has decided to use the causes/causes/effects structure for her essay on discrimination against women. Continue to help build the outline by filling in ideas for the missing elements.

Body ¶ 1 (Causes)

Topic: women are usually the primary caregiver in the family

Support: _____

_____

_____

_____

Body ¶ 2 (Causes)

Topic: _____

Support: politics has historically been male dominated

_____

_____

_____

Body ¶ 3 (Effects)

Topic: women have less of a voice in society

Support: women are 51% of population, but less than 5% of U.S. senators and members of Congress

_____

CONCLUSION

Your conclusion should begin by restating your thesis. Then summarize the main ideas and discuss your opinion about them. Try to give your readers something to think about after they have finished the essay. Include one or more of the following:

- Future prospects for the individuals discussed
- Remedies that might be pursued; for example, therapy to improve self-image
- Reasons why you believe change will happen naturally or with time.
- Reasons why you believe there will be no solutions in the foreseeable future.

Use results of studies, anecdotes, and personal examples in your conclusion.

Help finish this general outline for an essay on discrimination against women with the conclusion. Think about how this student could support her opinion and what she could give her reader to think about later.

Conclusion

Restatement of thesis: _____

_____

Your opinion: women have a different perspective on many aspects

of society, and that perspective is being undervalued or ignored.

Other points: _____

_____

_____

_____

What the reader should take away: _____

_____

_____

_____

3. Organizing a Cause-and-Effect Essay

Study this block diagram of a five-paragraph essay to plan a first draft of your essay. In your notebook, draw your own diagram and write your notes in each of its sections.

INTRODUCTION
Approach
Support
Thesis

BODY ¶ 1
Topic sentence
Support

BODY ¶ 2
Topic sentence
Support

BODY ¶ 3
Topic sentence
Support

CONCLUSION
Restatement of thesis
Summary of main ideas
Opinion

*Review your notes. Then write a **first draft** of your essay. Remember to write in complete sentences. Try to use some of the vocabulary and structures that you have practiced in this unit.*

C. Revising the First Draft

When you have finished writing your first draft, read it to a partner.

CHECKLIST FOR REVISING THE FIRST DRAFT

When you listen to your partner's essay and when you discuss your own, keep these questions in mind:

1. Does your introduction present a problem or state a commonly held belief?

2. Does your thesis statement mention the main points you intend to discuss?

3. Is the essay clearly organized, and is that organization consistent from paragraph to paragraph?

4. Do the body paragraphs deal with an effect for every cause, and vice versa?

5. Which types of support are used in the essay (SAFER)? Would other types of support help the essay? If so, which types?

6. Does the conclusion include the writer's opinion and give the reader something to think about?

After you have discussed your essay with a partner, you may want to reorganize your ideas, omit some, or add new ones.

*Now write a **second draft** that includes all of your additions and changes.*

D. Editing the Second Draft

After you have written a second draft, proofread your work for any errors and correct them. These guidelines and exercises should help.

1. Causal Connectors Using Transitions

Draw an arrow between the two ideas to show which is the cause and which is the effect: Cause ⟶ Effect *or* Effect ⟵ Cause. *Then use them in a sentence. Look back at the chart on page 96 to help you.*

1. a child is overweight ⟶ she or he is teased

   <u>When a child is overweight, this often results in the child being</u>

   <u>teased by other children.</u>

2. teasing   negative body image

   _____

   _____

3. low self-esteem   negative body image

   _____

   _____

4. eating disorders (anorexia, bulimia)   low self-esteem

   _____

   _____

5. emphasis on thinness in the media   self-consciousness about physical "imperfections"

   _____

   _____

6. self-consciousness   cosmetic surgery

   _____

   _____

7. increase in self-esteem   cosmetic surgery

   _____

   _____

2. Describing Research

Brief descriptions of research studies and their results can serve as support for thesis statements and main points made in an essay. There are a number of ways to incorporate the results of studies in your essay.

USE DIRECT SPEECH

Quote the researcher who performed the study:

Dr. Smith said, "We found that attractive people receive better treatment than unattractive people."

Synonyms for *said*: commented, stated, added, reported, emphasized, stressed

DESCRIBE WHAT THE RESEARCHER DID

Dr. Smith surveyed 100 people and found that 90% were dissatisfied with their appearance.

Dr. Smith discovered that almost no one was satisfied with his appearance.

USE AN EXPRESSION OF ATTRIBUTION

According to Dr. Smith, attractive people fared far better in studies than unattractive people.

USE THE PASSIVE VOICE

In a study by Dr. Smith, attractive people were found to have done much better in the job market than unattractive people.

LET THE RESEARCH SPEAK FOR ITSELF

Studies have found that people who were frequently teased between the ages of 8 and 16 developed negative body images.

Alternative phrases: Research has shown . . .
Research suggests . . .
Findings demonstrate . . .

In your notebook, write summaries of the information from two studies described in "How You See Yourself: Potential for Big Problems." Use one or more of the methods shown on page 108 for incorporating research findings.

1. Dr. Cash stated that once it is engraved in the brain, a negative body image influences feelings in countless situations. "For example, people who are self-conscious about some aspect of their appearance are more likely to interpret a negative remark in terms of it," he said.

   According to Dr. Cash, once it is engraved in the brain, a negative body image influences feelings in many different situations. He gave the example of people who are self-conscious about something in their appearance. His research shows that they "are more likely to interpret a negative remark in terms of it."

2. Dr. Robert Cleck, a psychologist at Dartmouth College, has devised an experiment that illustrates the way body image affects how people think. Using theatrical makeup, researchers put a scar on female subjects before their interaction with a stranger hired for the experiment. Without the subjects knowing it, however, the scar was removed before the face-to-face conversation with the stranger. Nevertheless, the women said that the stranger stared at the scar and made them feel uncomfortable about it.

3. "Hair loss is especially devastating to a young man in his 20s," said Dr. Cash, who is studying male baldness. "He thinks no one will love him and the door to his future is blocked. His friends tease him with names like 'Chrome Dome.' He constantly looks at other balding men to compare himself," Dr. Cash said, usually reinforcing a negative image in the process.

4. In a recent experiment, Dr. Cash surveyed 145 men about their emotional and behavioral reactions to balding. Of these, 42 had a full head of hair, 63 had visible thinning, and 4 had extensive hair loss. "The men who had not yet lost any hair said they would be very distressed if they did," Dr. Cash said. "Half of the men with modest hair loss were worried about it," he continued, "whereas three-fourths of those with extensive hair loss were distressed and preoccupied with their condition."

In a small group, read your summaries aloud and discuss them. Give helpful criticism about the ways in which the writer describes the research.

E. Preparing the Final Draft

Reread your second draft and correct any errors you find. Put a check (✓) in each space as you edit your essay for these points. Then write your corrected final version.

> ## CHECKLIST FOR EDITING THE SECOND DRAFT
>
> _____ **clear causal connections with appropriate transitions, punctuated correctly**
>
> _____ **research described in a variety of ways**

 V Additional Writing Opportunities

Write about one of the following topics.

1. Many have claimed that the fashion, cosmetics, and advertising industries are promoting an impossible standard of beauty, one that very few people can meet. What are some possible reasons for their promotion of an unrealistic standard of beauty? What are the effects on people and society?

2. Recently, a well-known female opera singer was fired from a production because the opera company said that she was too fat to fit into her costume. Some years ago, a broadcast news reporter was fired for not being sufficiently attractive. Do employers have the right to demand that their employees fit a stereotyped notion of attractiveness if the employees are, in all other respects, good at their jobs? Is it different for different occupations? If so, give examples.

3. Daniel Hamermesh, a professor of economics at the University of Texas at Austin, and Amy Parker, one of his students, found that on student evaluations of teaching, attractive professors consistently get higher scores by a significant margin than their less attractive colleagues. These findings, they say, raise serious questions about the use of student evaluations as a valid measure of teaching quality. If students do indeed discriminate based on attractiveness, should schools eliminate teaching evaluations or, at least, give them less importance?

6 Two Theories of Personality Types

WRITING A COMPARISON AND CONTRAST ESSAY

In this unit you will practice:
- developing introductions
- assessing the value of a theory

Editing focus:
- clauses for comparison, contrast, and concession
- transitions for comparison and contrast

I Fluency Practice: Freewriting and Speaking

How much can you know about someone from looking at him/her? Think about the two men in the photograph above. What type of person do you think each man is? Why?

Now think of someone whom you have met recently. What conclusions did you draw about that person in the first few minutes after you met? What made you draw these conclusions? In your notebook, describe the person you met and the conclusions you came to about his/her character as best as you can. Discuss your answers with a partner.

111

Reading for Writing, Part A

This article discusses William Sheldon's controversial theories on the connection between a person's appearance and personality.

APPEARANCE AND PERSONALITY: SHELDON'S THEORY OF BODY TYPE AND TEMPERAMENT

by James and Tyra Arraj

In the 1940s, William Sheldon (1898–1977), an American psychologist, proposed a theory that particular body types, or somatotypes, are associated with particular personality characteristics. For his study of the human physique,[1] Dr. Sheldon looked at 4,000 photographs of college-age men in front, back and side views. By carefully examining these photos, he determined that there are three fundamental components of physical form. When mixed together in different combinations, the result is a set of seven possible somatotypes.

Sheldon worked out ways to measure the three components of physical form and to express them numerically. Consequently, every human body could be described in terms of these numbers, and two independent observers could arrive at very similar results when classifying a person's body type. Sheldon named these basic elements endomorphy, mesomorphy and ectomorphy. He drew a triangular diagram on which he plotted the different extremes of body types.

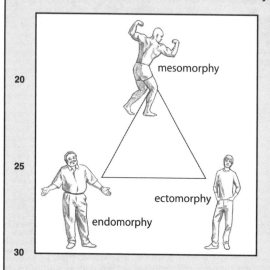

Endomorphy is centered on the abdomen and the whole digestive system. Mesomorphy is focused on the muscles and the circulatory system. Ectomorphy is related to the brain and the nervous system.

Every person has all three components in his/her physical makeup, however, just as we all have digestive, circulatory, and nervous systems. No one is endomorphic without also being to some degree mesomorphic and ectomorphic. For example, Sheldon found that the hefty muscular person was quite common, as were the muscular thin person and the person who was spread out and round without being muscular at all. Sheldon devised a scale to evaluate the

---

1. *physique:* size and shape of a person's body

extent to which a person had each component. The scale ranges from
35 1 to 7—with 1 signifying a minimum degree of a component and 7
signifying the maximum.

The classification of body types was not Sheldon's ultimate[2] goal.
He wanted to resolve the age-old[3] question of whether our body type is
connected with the way people behave. In short, he wanted to explore the
40 link between body and temperament.

Temperament refers to personality and emotional makeup—the way
people eat and sleep, laugh and cry, speak and walk. Sheldon's system
for determining the basic components of temperament was much like
the one he used for determining body types. He did in-depth interviews
45 of several hundred people to find traits that he could use to describe
the basic elements of behavior.
He found three and named
them similarly to their physical
counterparts: endotonia, mesotonia
and ectotonia.

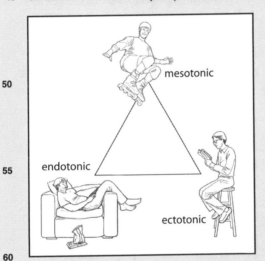

Endotonia is seen in the love
of relaxation, comfort, food, and
people. Mesotonia is centered on
assertiveness and a love of action.
Ectotonia focuses on privacy,
restraint[4] and a highly developed
self-awareness.

Like physical traits, Sheldon
devised a way of numerically rating
these personality traits. His system
was based on a checklist of sixty
characteristics. The extremes can also be plotted on a triangular diagram.
The "7-1-1" person is extremely endotonic, the "1-7-1" person is extreme
mesotonic, and the "1-1-7" person is extremely ectotonic.

65 As his terminology implies, Sheldon found a strong correspondence
between the ectomorphic body type and the ectotonic temperament,
between the mesomorphic body type and the mesotonic temperament,
and between the endomorphic body type and the endotonic personality.
But, just as a person's body type has all three elements, so, too, does a
70 person's temperament.

---

2. *ultimate:* final
3. *age-old:* ancient; of long standing
4. *restraint:* reserve; moderation in action or expression

A. General Understanding, Part A

1. Categorizing Somatotypes and Personality Traits

Match the physical and personality traits associated with each somatotype by filling in the chart below.

Physical traits

hard, muscular body

thin, delicate build

soft, round body

Personality traits

active	introverted
combative	quiet
courageous	relaxed
good-humored	sensitive
	tolerant

Somatotype	Physical traits	Personality traits
1. Endomorphic		
2. Mesomorphic		
3. Ectomorphic		

2. Determining Your Somatotype

Look at the Physical Traits column in the chart on page 114. For each body type, rate yourself below. Give yourself a number from 1 (lowest degree present) to 7 (highest degree present) for each category. Then place yourself on the triangular diagram. Compare and discuss your results with a partner.

The degree to which
I am endomorphic: _____

The degree to which
I am mesomorphic: _____

The degree to which
I am ectomorphic: _____

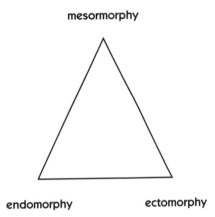

3. Determining Your Personality Type

*Fill out this temperament profile for yourself. For each item in the chart, give a number from 1 (very little or no preference) to 7 (strong preference) for **every** possible answer.*

SIMPLIFIED SCALE OF TEMPERAMENT

	Endotonia 1–7	Mesotonia 1–7	Ectotonia 1–7
1. When troubled, I seek out . . .	people _____	action _____	solitude _____
2. I prefer . . .	physical comfort _____	physical adventure _____	privacy _____
3. The time of my life I favor is . . .	childhood _____	early adulthood _____	later years _____
4. What would bother me most would be . . .	being cut off from other people _____	being closed off in small places _____	being exposed to endless noise _____
5. When in a group, I like to . . .	mingle _____	take charge _____	take off _____
6. I prefer to . . .	let things take their course _____	do things _____	observe what is going on _____
7. The thing I like most is . . .	eating _____	exercise _____	time to myself _____

Look at each vertical answer column in the chart on page 115 separately. Look at the numbers you gave each possibility and figure out an average score. Write your average scores in the categories below. Then place yourself on the triangular diagram. Compare and discuss your results with a partner.

The degree to which I am endotonic: _____

The degree to which I am mesotonic: _____

The degree to which I am ectotonic: _____

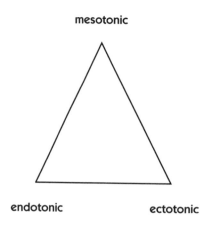

4. Comparing Body and Personality Types

Look again at the ratings you gave yourself in Exercise 2 (body type) and Exercise 3 (temperament). Are your numbers for endomorphy and endotonia similar? For mesomorphy and mesotonia? For ectomorphy and ectotonia? Write your thoughts about how well your results correlate below. Discuss your thoughts with a partner.

B. Working with Language

1. Understanding Prefixes and Suffixes

Match the following prefixes and suffix to the correct definition.

_____ 1. *ecto-*   a. body

_____ 2. *endo-*   b. intermediate

_____ 3. *meso-*   c. in, into

_____ 4. *-morph*   d. shape, form, structure

_____ 5. *somato-*   e. external, outer

2. Building Words with Prefixes and Suffixes

Look at the underlined word in each sentence. Write the meaning of the word in the blank. Then write the meaning of the prefix or suffix.

1. George is quite shy and <u>introverted</u>. He hardly ever socializes with other students.

   introverted means _____

   intro- probably means _____

   -vert probably means _____

2. George's twin brother, Alex, is just the opposite. He is friendly and <u>extroverted</u>. Whenever I see him at a party, he is always talking to lots of people.

   extroverted means _____

   extro- probably means _____

3. George and Alex came to my party last month. Alex <u>circulated</u> all evening, talking to some people for a while and then moving on and talking to others. George just stayed on the couch and talked to one or two people. He didn't circulate at all.

   circulate means _____

   circu- probably means _____

4. Usually, George doesn't go to parties. He always says that he is sick. I think his illnesses are <u>psychosomatic</u>. No one can have that many colds in one year!

psychosomatic means _____

psycho- probably means _____

5. Have you seen George yet? What a <u>metamorphosis</u>! He grew about three inches over the summer. He's very thin now and much more social. It's as if he is a different person!

metamorphosis means _____

meta- probably means _____

 II ## Reading for Writing, Part B

Other psychologists have developed different approaches to typology, or personality typing. Read about the Myers-Briggs Type Indicator (MBTI).

A HOLISTIC APPROACH TO PERSONALITY ANALYSIS: THE MYERS-BRIGGS TYPE INDICATOR

Among the most widely used psychological types are those developed by the Swiss psychologist Carl Jung (1875–1961). His typology emerges from his deep, holistic[1] philosophy about psychology and people. He viewed the ultimate psychological task as the process of individuation,[2]
5 based on the strengths and limitations of one's psychological type.

Isabel Briggs Myers and her mother, Katharine Cook Briggs, developed the Myers-Briggs Type Indicator based on Jung's typology. Underlying these typologies are four personality traits, or functions:

Extroversion–Introversion: Do you recharge your energy via external
10 contact and activity (extroversion) or by spending time in your inner space (introversion)?

Intuition–Sensing: Do you rely on your inner voice (intuition) or observation (sensing)?

continued

---

1. *holistic:* emphasizing the importance of the whole and interdependence of the parts.
2. *individuation:* Jung's term for the process of becoming a complete human being who has developed all aspects of "self."

Thinking–Feeling: When making decisions, what do you rely on
15 most—your thoughts or your feelings?
　　Judgment–Perception: Do you tend to set schedules and organize
　　your life (judgment) or do you tend to leave options open and see what
　　happens (perception)?
　　People fill out self-assessment questionnaires to determine the degree
20 of each trait in his / her personality. The first trait defines the source and
direction of a person's energy expression. The extrovert has a source and
direction of energy mainly in the external world, while the introvert has a
source of energy mainly in the internal world. No one is only introverted or
extroverted, but one side is usually dominant.
25　　The second function defines the method of a person's information
perception. Sensing means that a person believes mainly in information
he receives from the external world. Intuition means that a person
believes mainly in information he receives from the internal or imaginative
world. The short quiz on sensation and intuition illustrates the differences.

	Intuition	Sensation
I tend to . . .	a. get excited about the future	b. savor the present moment
When I have definite plans, . . .	a. I feel somewhat tied down	b. I am comfortable with them
If I worked for a manufacturer, I would prefer to do...	a. research and design	b. production and distribution
I am inclined to . . .	a. get involved in many projects at once	b. do one thing at a time
If people were to complain about me, they would say . . .	a. I have my head in the clouds	b. I am in a rut
People would call me . . .	a. imaginative	b. realistic
When I find myself in a new situation, I am more interested in . . .	a. what could happen	b. what is happening

continued

30 The third function defines how a person processes information. Thinking means that a person makes decisions mainly through logic. Feeling means that, as a rule, he makes a decision based on emotion.

The fourth category defines how a person implements or uses information that he has processed. Judging means that a person 35 organizes all his life events and acts strictly according to his plans. Perceiving means that he is inclined to improvise and seek alternatives.

The different combinations of the traits determine a type. There are sixteen possible types. Every type has a name (or formula) according to the combination of criteria. Letters stand for each trait. For example: ISTJ 40 is Introvert Sensing Thinking Judging, or ENFP is Extrovert Intuitive (N) Feeling Perceiving.

A type formula and a quantitative measure of expression of each criterion (strength of the preference) can be determined using the type inventory. Then a corresponding type description can be derived, as shown below.

ENFP: The ENFP takes her energy from the outer world of actions and spoken words. She prefers dealing with patterns and possibilities, particularly for people, and makes decisions based on personal values. Her life is flexible, following new insights and possibilities as they arise. She is creative and insightful, often seeking to try new ideas that can be of benefit to people. She may sometimes neglect details and planning, but she enjoys work that involves experimentation and variety, working toward a general goal.

A. General Understanding, Part B

1. Categorizing Personality Traits

Look at the groups of words. From your understanding of the reading, label each group according to which personality function pair it describes. Then label each column within the group according to its individual function. Add one trait to each function. Discuss your additions with your classmates.

E I = extroversion–introversion
N S = intuition–sensing
T F = thinking–feeling
J P = judgment–perception

1. __EI__

__E__	__I__
social	private
expressive	quiet
interaction	concentration
action before thought	thought before action
unpredictable	_stable_

2. _____

_____	_____
analyzing	sympathizing
objective	subjective
logical	personal
criticism	appreciation
_____	_____

3. _____

_____	_____
decide	explore
organize	inquire
firmness	flexibility
control	spontaneity
_____	_____

4. _____

_____	_____
facts	possibilities
experience	novelty
present	future
realism	idealism
_____	_____

2. Determining Typology

Look at the categories of traits / functions in Exercise 1 again and decide which ones apply to you. What is your type formula? Discuss your conclusions with a partner. Then compose a paragraph in your notebook describing a person with your formula. Follow the model of the ENFP formula on page 120.

3. Comparing Results

Do your results in the Sheldon system match your results in the Myers-Briggs system? What could explain the differences? Discuss your answers with a partner.

B. Open for Discussion

Discuss these questions in a small group. Then choose one question and summarize the group's discussion of it in your notebook.

1. Have you ever taken a personality quiz in a magazine or on the Internet? Do you think the results reflected who you are as a person? Why do you think personality quizzes are so popular?

2. What is the value of personality typing for the individual? How could a person use that information to his or her advantage? What are some possible disadvantages to knowing your own personality type?

3. How might prospective employers use personality assessments to determine whether someone is a good candidate for a position? In what fields might personality assessments work best? Why?

4. What do you think about the Sheldon and Myers-Briggs theories of personality? Does one theory seem better than the other? Why? Which describes you better? Why?

III ◆ Prewriting Activities

A. Sheldon's Theory

1. Summarizing Sheldon's Theory

Look back at the reading on pages 112–113. Fill in the chart below.

SOMATOTYPES AND PERSONALITY

When developed	1940's
Methodology used in determining somatotypes	Sheldon examined photographs of 4,000 college-age men. He devised a system of measuring the components that made up their body types.
Number of types	
Name and primary characteristics of each body type	
Method used to link body and personality types	
Number of personality types	
Name and primary characteristics of each personality type	
Total number of personality types that can be derived using this theory	

2. Analyzing Sheldon's Theory

Do you think Sheldon's theory could be accurately applied to the general population? Why or why not? In your notebook, write down what you believe to be good or bad about the theory. Give examples of situations in which it could or could not be accurately applied.

B. The Myers-Briggs Theory

1. Summarizing the Myers-Briggs Theory

Look back at the reading on pages 118–120. Fill in the chart below.

MEYERS-BRIGGS THEORY

Basis of theory	Jung's philosophy and psychology about how an individual develops all aspects of the "self."
Methodology used in determining personality type	
Number of personality traits / functions	
Names of personality traits / functions	
Total number of personality types that can be derived using this theory	
How results are obtained	

2. Analyzing the Myers-Briggs Theory

Do you think that this theory could be accurately applied to the general population? Why or why not? In your notebook, write down what you believe to be good or bad about this theory. Give examples of situations in which it could not be accurately applied.

IV Structured Writing Focus

YOUR TASK

Write a five-paragraph essay comparing and contrasting William Sheldon's Body Type and Personality Assessment with the Myers-Briggs Typology Index. Include the following in your essay: the method of development—whether it is based on theory or scientific experimentation; the number of possible types; the range and method of application; the credibility of the theory.

ALTERNATIVE TASK: Write a five-paragraph essay comparing and contrasting one other theory of personality with either the Sheldon Body Type and Personality Assessment or the Myers-Briggs Index. For example, do research on a theory such as Type A / Type B Personalities, Handwriting Analysis, or Astrological Profiles. Include the following in your essay: the method of development—whether it is based on theory or scientific experimentation; the number of possible categories; the range and method of application; the credibility of the theory.

A. Starting to Write

1. Brainstorming

Fill in the typology questionnaire. Answer the questions with yes or no for each theory based on your understanding of the readings.

TYPOLOGY QUESTIONNAIRE

	Theory 1	Theory 2
1. Are the results the same every time the theory is applied?	no	no
2. Can it be applied to the general population?		
3. Does it work for different cultural backgrounds?		
4. Are the results based on scientific experiments?		
5. Are the results based on self-reports?		

continued on next page

Two Theories of Personality Types   125

	Theory 1	Theory 2
6. Are the results based on the theorist's own observations?		
7. Is the theory useful for hiring suitable personnel for a job?		
8. Is the theory useful for helping people find business partners, friends, or love interests?		
9. Is the theory useful for helping people understand themselves better?		
10. Do you think two independent researchers using this theory would always come up with the same results?		

2. Comparing and Contrasting Theories

Do a point-by-point comparison of theories by filling in the chart with the similarities and differences for each point of comparison.

Points of comparison	Similarities	Differences
Method of development: based on theory or scientific experimentation		
Degree of differentiation: Number of categories		
Range and method of application		
Credibility		

B. Preparing the First Draft

1. Introductory Paragraphs for Comparison and Contrast Essays

A comparison and contrast essay is not merely a list of similarities and differences. It is either

an evaluation of the relative merits of the two things (for example, Theory A has a far greater range of applications than Theory B).

or

an argument that the similarities and differences have a larger significance (such as demonstrating the effect of having a particular personality type on one's health or chances for success).

The approach of your essay should be clear in the introductory paragraph.

Read this introductory paragraph comparing and contrasting Sheldon's theory with the Myers-Briggs theory. Then answer the questions that follow.

Why do we do the things we do? William Sheldon's Body Type and Temperament theory and the Myers-Briggs Type Indicator (MBTI) are two attempts to answer this question. These two theories are very similar in their origins. Neither of them is based on controlled scientific studies. Sheldon hoped to show that there is a link between people's personalities and their physical appearance. The MBTI, on the other hand, is based on the idea that people's personalities are not physical but psychological. The MBTI fits all personalities into the philosophical categories developed by Carl Jung, which rely on Jung's clinical observations and subjective memories. Both Sheldon's theory and the MBTI claim that assumptions and predictions can be made about a person based on his or her personality type. Although the typology of each system is different, their common assertion that their own system can predict behavior is fundamentally flawed and potentially harmful.

1. Does this introduction have a hook? If so, what is it?

2. What is the thesis statement?

3. What is the writer's attitude toward these theories?

4. What words in the paragraph help the writer explain similarities? What words highlight differences?

5. How does the thesis statement point to similarities and contrasts at the same time?

2. Organizing Your Essay

Comparison and contrast essays can be organized in several ways. Study the block diagrams of two possible structures to plan a first draft of your comparison and contrast essay. Decide how you would like to organize your essay. Then, in your notebook, draw your own diagram and write your notes in each of its sections.

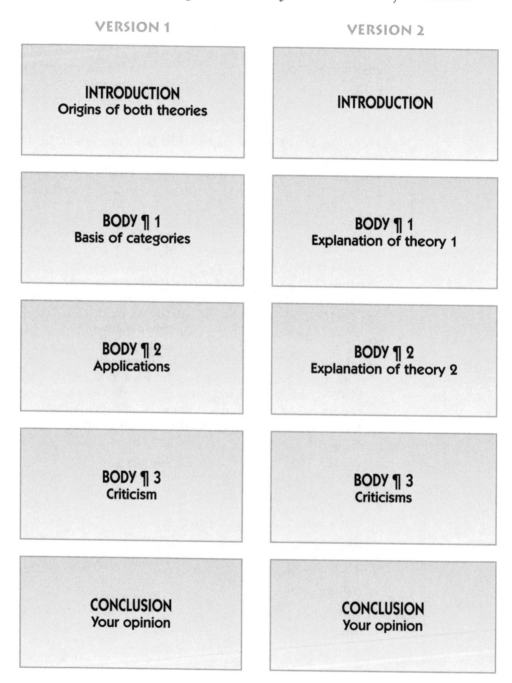

VERSION 1

INTRODUCTION
Origins of both theories

BODY ¶ 1
Basis of categories

BODY ¶ 2
Applications

BODY ¶ 3
Criticism

CONCLUSION
Your opinion

VERSION 2

INTRODUCTION

BODY ¶ 1
Explanation of theory 1

BODY ¶ 2
Explanation of theory 2

BODY ¶ 3
Criticisms

CONCLUSION
Your opinion

*Now write a **first draft** of your essay. Try to use some of the vocabulary and structures that you have practiced in this unit.*

C. Revising the First Draft

When you have finished writing the first draft, read it to a partner.

CHECKLIST FOR REVISING THE FIRST DRAFT

When you listen to your partner's essay and when you discuss your own, keep these questions in mind:

1. Does the introduction clearly state the two theories being compared / contrasted?

2. Does the introduction give the reader an idea of the approach to the topic that the writer is going to take?

3. Does each body paragraph focus on one element of the comparison?

4. Does the writer use a variety of expressions to show comparison and contrast?

5. Is the writer's opinion in the conclusion? Is this opinion supported by the body paragraphs?

After discussing your essay with a partner, some reorganization may be necessary.

*Now write a **second draft** that includes all of your changes.*

D. Editing the Second Draft

1. Clauses of Comparison, Contrast, and Concession

Use clauses of comparison, contrast, and concession to help your reader follow your argument and to improve coherence in your comparison and contrast writing.

COMPARISON: SIMILARITY

just as   in the same way as/that   similar to   like

In the same way that Sheldon's theory uses self-reporting as an assessment tool, the MBTI depends on an individual's honest answers to a series of questions.

Similar to Sheldon's use of self-reporting, the MBTI depends on an individual's honest answers to a series of questions.

CONTRAST: DIFFERENCE

while/whereas   in contrast to   unlike

While Type A personalities are driven, ambitious people, Type Bs tend to be less high-strung and more relaxed.

Unlike people with Type A personalities, Type Bs tend to be relaxed and easy-going.

CONCESSION

Use concession language to recognize one aspect of a topic before highlighting another aspect of it.

although   even though   though   despite the fact that

Even though <u>Type As are more prone to heart disease,</u>	they are <u>also more likely to be successful</u> in high-powered positions.
RECOGNIZE ONE ASPECT	HIGHLIGHT ANOTHER ASPECT
Type Bs <u>can be very successful</u> in their work lives	**despite the fact that** they <u>tend to be relaxed and easy-going</u>.
RECOGNIZE ONE ASPECT	HIGHLIGHT ANOTHER ASPECT

Combine the sentences using a clause of comparison, contrast, or concession. Compare your sentences with a partner.

1. a. Numerologists often use the number of letters in a person's name to create a personality profile.

   b. Astrologers use people's birth date to create personality profiles for them.

   _____

   _____

2. a. Many people enjoy taking personality tests in magazines.

   b. Few people have much faith in personality tests in magazines.

   _____

   _____

3. a. Sheldon's endomorphs are lively, social people who enjoy parties.

   b. Myers-Briggs' extroverts enjoy human contact and social situations.

   _____

   _____

4. a. Serious astrologers base their analyses on careful study and observation.

   b. Astrologers are not trained scientists and have no expertise in drawing larger conclusions from their observations.

   _____

   _____

   _____

5. a. Handwriting analysis claims to examine personality based on a physical manifestation of subconscious temperament.

   b. Sheldon claimed to analyze personality based on the physical manifestation of subconscious temperament.

   _____

   _____

   _____

   _____

2. Transitional Expressions Between Sentences

When these transitions occur between two independent clauses, they must be preceded by a period or a semicolon.

SIMILARITY

likewise   similarly   in the same way

Sheldon's typology has been criticized for being unreliable; **in the same way**, researchers devalue the MBTI because they cannot duplicate results.

DIFFERENCE

on the other hand   conversely   in contrast   however

Sheldon's typology is based on somatotypes, which can be observed; **in contrast**, the MBTI relies solely on self-assessment.

Combine the sentences using a transitional expression. Compare your sentences with a partner.

1. a. Numerologists use numbers to chart a person's personality.

   b. Astrologers use birthdates to chart personalities.

   _____

   _____

2. a. The western zodiac describes people's personalities in terms of animals, occupations, and objects.

   b. The Chinese zodiac describes people's personalities only in terms of animals.

   _____

   _____

3. a. In Asia, the meaning of the Chinese characters in a person's name reflects the parents' hopes for the child's future.

   b. In western countries, children's names often reflect the parents' hopes for their children's future.

   _____

   _____

4. a. The MBTI depends on people's honesty and their ability to accurately assess their own attitudes and behaviors.

   b. Astrology depends on fixed and confirmable data about a person's birth and the positions of different celestial bodies.

   _____

   _____

5. a. Handwriting analysis strives to tell people something about their own characters.

   b. Astrology hopes to give people insight into their own potential and limits.

   _____

   _____

E. Preparing the Final Draft

Reread your second draft and correct any errors you find. Put a check (✓) in each space as you edit for these points. Then write your corrected final version.

CHECKLIST FOR EDITING THE SECOND DRAFT

_____ clauses of comparison, contrast, and concession

_____ transitional expressions between sentences

Additional Writing Opportunities

Write about one of the following topics.

1. You are the administrator for a new, large urban hospital. You have been asked to select a team of people to help you run the hospital. Decide whether to use the Myers-Briggs Index or Sheldon's Body Types and Personality Assessment or another method of personality type assessment in order to select the members of your team. Explain why you chose that method and how it will help you select the most qualified people.

2. Compare two methods for losing weight or improving your body. Explain their similarities and differences. What criticisms have been made of each method? What type of person do you think each method would appeal to?

3. Compare two Internet dating services. Discuss the value of their interviews, questionnaires, and personality profiles in terms of their effectiveness. Are their claims of success supported by evidence? What criticisms have been made of their methods for matching people? Do you believe these criticisms are valid? Why or why not?

4. Write an essay about the differences between "left-brain" and "right-brain" people. Go online and do some research on the topic. What are the major differences? What are the similarities? What research has been done to determine these similarities and differences? Are the results convincing? Do the results vary from culture to culture?

THE KITE RUNNER

WRITING A LITERARY ANALYSIS ESSAY

In this unit you will practice:
- analyzing mood
- summarizing a story
- understanding plot devices
- writing about symbols
- organizing an introduction for a literary analysis essay
- using quotes as support in an essay
- integrating quotes with text

Editing focus:
- present and past unreal conditionals

I   Fluency Practice: Freewriting

Who was your best friend when you were young? What kinds of things did you enjoy doing together? Did you ever fly kites together? Were you ever in a contest together? Were you ever jealous of your friend? Why or why not? How has that friendship affected your life?

Write for ten minutes. Try to express yourself as well as you can. Don't worry about mistakes. Share your writing with a partner.

II **Reading for Writing**

In *The Kite Runner*, Khaled Hosseini tells the story of a privileged young boy named Amir growing up in Afghanistan during a time of political turmoil. In this excerpt, Amir and his servant, a young boy named Hassan, are talking about a dream Hassan had the night before.

THE KITE RUNNER
by Khaled Hosseini

The next morning, as he brewed black tea for breakfast, Hassan told me he'd had a dream. "We were at Ghargha Lake, you, me, Father, Agha sahib, Rahim Khan, and thousands of other people," he said. "It was warm and
5 sunny, and the lake was clear like a mirror. But no one was swimming because they said a monster had come to the lake. It was swimming at the bottom, waiting."

He poured me a cup and added sugar, blew on it a few times. Put it before me. "So everyone is scared to get in the water, and
10 suddenly you kick off your shoes. Amir agha, and take off your shirt. 'There's no monster', you say. 'I'll show you all.' And before anyone can stop you, you dive into the water, start swimming away. I follow you in and we're both swimming."

"But you can't swim."

15 Hassan laughed. "It's a dream, Amir agha, you can do anything. Anyway, everyone is screaming, 'Get out! Get out! But we just swim in the cold water. We make it way out to the middle of the lake and we stop swimming. We turn toward the shore and wave to the people. They look small
20 like ants, but we can hear them clapping. They see now. There is no monster, just water. They change the name of the lake after that, and call it the 'Lake of Amir and Hassan, Sultans of Kabul,' and we get to charge people money for swimming in it."

25 "So what does it mean?" I said.

He coated my naan with marmalade, placed it on a plate. "I don't know. I was hoping you could tell me."

"Well, it's a dumb dream. Nothing happens in it."

"Father says dreams always mean something."

30 I sipped some tea. "Why don't you ask him, then? He's so smart," I said, more curtly than I had intended. I hadn't slept all night. My neck and back were like coiled springs, and my eyes stung. Still, I had been mean to Hassan. I almost apologized, then didn't. Hassan understood I was just
35 nervous. Hassan always understood about me.

Upstairs, I could hear the water running in Baba's bathroom.

Agha sahib: Amir's father

Rahim Khan: a family friend

agha: a title of respect in Afghanistan

Sultans of Kabul: ancient rulers of the city of Kabul, Afghanistan

curtly: impolitely

like coiled springs: tense

my eyes stung: my eyes hurt

Baba: father

A. General Understanding

Write answers to these questions using information from the reading to support your opinions. Then share your answers with a partner.

1. What happens in Hassan's dream? What do you think the dream means? What is the monster at the bottom of the lake?

2. Who seems the braver of the two–Hassan or Amir? Why do you think so?

3. Look at the end of the excerpt and try to predict the rest of the story. Why is Amir nervous? Will Hassan be upset with Amir? How does Amir feel about his father?

B. Literary Analysis

Like most other subjects, literature has its own set of terms and expressions to describe it or discuss it. Here are some of the more common ones:

1. The **plot** is a series of events chosen and arranged by an author to elicit a particular emotional response from a reader. It is the plan of a literary work.

2. A **narrative** is an account of a series of events or facts given in order. It is a story or a telling of a story. Unlike a plot, the events told are not arranged to elicit a particular response from a reader or listener.

3. The **mood** of a literary piece refers to the atmosphere in the story—how the writer makes the reader feel at any given point in the story.

4. The **theme** of a literary piece is the subject of the work and how the author feels about that subject. For example, the subject of The Kite Runner might be Hassan. The theme would be what Amir learned about himself through his relationship with Hassan.

5. **Tension** refers to a state of stress produced by anxiety or conflict. In writing, building tension generally leads to a climax.

6. The **climax** is the point of greatest emotional intensity in a plot.

7. A **figure of speech** is a literary device often used by authors to associate or compare distinct things. A figure of speech generally creates an image in the mind of the reader, different from the literal meaning. **Figurative language** is language that uses figures of speech.

8. An example of a figure of speech is a **symbol**. A symbol is something that represents or stands for something else, generally something larger or more complex. For example, a flag represents a particular country. That flag can be a symbol for the characteristics of the country.

Continue reading The Kite Runner *and then complete the exercise that follows.*

In the next part of the story, Amir and his servant, Hassan, are about to take part in a kite contest. The strings of the kites are coated in glass to enable them to cut the strings of other kites in the contest. The glass strings also cut the hands of the kite flyers. The kite that remains flying the longest wins the contest, and the boy who can endure the most pain to defeat his enemies is considered a hero. Amir's father is watching from a rooftop.

The streets glistened with fresh snow and the sky was a blameless blue. Snow blanketed every rooftop and weighed on the branches of the stunted mulberry trees
40 that lined our street. Overnight, snow had nudged its way into every crack and gutter. I squinted against the blinding white when Hassan and I stepped through the wrought-iron gates. Ali shut the gates behind us. I heard him utter a prayer under his breath—he always said a prayer when his
45 son left the house.

glistened: shined

I had never seen so many people on our street. Kids were flinging snowballs, squabbling, chasing one another, giggling. Kite fighters were huddling with their spool holders, making last-minute preparations. From adjacent
50 streets, I could hear laughter and chatter. Already, rooftops were jammed with spectators reclining in lawn chairs, hot tea steaming from thermoses, and music blared from cassette players. I turned my gaze to our rooftop, found Baba and Rahim Khan sitting on a bench, both dressed in
55 wool sweaters, sipping tea. Baba waved. I couldn't tell if he was waving at me or Hassan.

squabbling: arguing
huddling: crowding closely
spool: string holder

"We should get started," Hassan said. He wore black rubber snow boots and a bright green chapan over a thick sweater and faded corduroy pants. Sunlight washed over
60 his face, and, in it, I saw how well the pink scar above his lip had healed.

Suddenly I wanted to withdraw. Pack it all in, go back home. What was I thinking? Why was I putting myself through this, when I already knew the outcome? Baba was
65 on the roof, watching me. I felt his glare on me like the heat of a blistering sun. This would be failure on a grand scale, even for me.

pack it all in: quit; give up
putting myself through this: forcing myself to do something difficult
glare: fierce look or stare
blistering: burning

"I'm not sure I want to fly a kite today," I said.

"It's a beautiful day," Hassan said.

70 I shifted on my feet. Tried to peel my gaze away from our rooftop. "I don't know. Maybe we should go home."

Then he stepped toward me and, in a low voice, said

peel my gaze away from: stop looking at

something that scared me a little. "Remember, Amir agha. There's no monster, just a beautiful day." How could I be
75 such an <u>open book</u> to him when, half the time, I had no idea <u>what was milling around in his head</u>? I was the one who went to school, the one who could read, write. I was the smart one. Hassan couldn't read a first-grade textbook but <u>he'd read me plenty</u>. That was a little <u>unsettling</u>, but
80 also sort of comfortable to have someone who always knew what you needed.

"No monster," I said, feeling a little better, to my own surprise.

He smiled. "No monster."

85 "Are you sure?"

He closed his eyes. Nodded.

I looked to the kids <u>scampering</u> down the street, flinging snowballs. "It is a beautiful day, isn't it?"

"Let's fly," he said.

90 It occurred to me then that maybe Hassan had made up his dream. Was that possible? I decided it wasn't. Hassan wasn't that smart. *I* wasn't that smart. But made up or not, the silly dream had lifted some of my anxiety. Maybe I *should* take off my shirt, take a swim in the lake. Why not?

95 "Let's do it," I said.

Hassan's face brightened. "Good," he said.

continued

open book: a person who can't hide his feelings

what was milling around in his head: what he was thinking

he'd read me plenty: he understood me well

unsettling: uncomfortable

scampering: running playfully

Analyze the mood of the reading. Write answers to these questions using information from the reading to support your opinions. Then share your answers with a partner.

1. How does the author describe the day? How does his description make you feel? Which images are positive? Which are negative? How do the images add to the mood of the story?

2. How do the spectators in the story feel? Hassan? Amir? How do you know? Which lines in the story support your opinions?

3. How does Amir feel about his *baba,* his father? Which lines in the story reveal this?

4. How does Hassan comfort Amir? Why does this surprise Amir? How does Hassan's advice make Amir feel?

5. How did Hassan's dream help Amir? Did Hassan make up the dream?

6. What does Amir mean when he says, "Maybe I should take off my shirt, take a swim in the lake. Why not?"

III Prewriting Activities

Read the concluding excerpt from The Kite Runner. *Then complete the exercises that follow.*

This excerpt describes the kite contest and reveals the winner. It also helps us understand Amir's relationship with his father and with his servant and friend, Hassan.

Hassan lifted our kite, red with yellow borders. He licked his finger and held it up, tested the wind, then
100 ran in its direction—on those rare occasions we flew kites in the summer, he'd kick up the dust to see which way the wind blew it. The spool rolled in my hands until Hassan stopped, about fifty feet away. He held the kite high over his head, like an Olympic athlete
105 showing his gold medal. I <u>jerked</u> the string twice, our usual signal, and Hassan <u>tossed</u> the kite.

jerked: pulled on
tossed: threw

I took a deep breath, exhaled, and pulled on the string. Within a minute, my kite was rocketing to the sky. It made a sound like a paper bird flapping its
110 wings. Hassan clapped his hands, whistled, and ran back to me. I handed him the spool, holding on to the string, and he <u>spun</u> it quickly to roll the loose string back on.

spun: turned

At least two dozen kites
115 already hung in the sky, like paper sharks <u>roaming for prey</u>. Within an hour, the number doubled, and red, blue, and yellow kites <u>glided</u>
120 and spun in the sky. A cold breeze <u>wafted</u> through my hair. The wind was perfect for kite flying, blowing just hard enough to give some
125 lift, make the sweeps easier. Next to me, Hassan held the spool, his hands already bloodied by the string.

roaming for prey: looking for something to attack

glided: moved smoothly

wafted: moved gently

Soon, <u>the cutting</u> started and the first of the defeated kites whirled out of control. They fell from
130 the sky like shooting stars with brilliant, rippling tails, showering the neighborhoods below with prizes for the kite runners. I could hear the runners now, <u>hollering</u> as they ran the streets. Someone shouted reports of a fight breaking out two streets down.

the cutting: the kite strings cutting each other

hollering: shouting

135 I kept <u>stealing glances</u> at Baba sitting on the roof, wondered what he was thinking. Was he cheering for me? Or did a part of him enjoy watching me fail? That was the thing about kite flying: <u>Your mind drifted</u> with the kite.

140 They were coming down all over the place now, the kites, and I was still flying. I was still flying. My eyes kept <u>wandering</u> over to Baba, bundled up in his wool sweater. Was he surprised I had lasted as long as I had?

Up and down the streets, kite runners were 145 returning triumphantly, their captured kites held high. They showed them off to their parents, their friends. But they all knew the best was yet to come. The biggest prize of all was still flying.

Within another hour, the number of <u>surviving</u> kites 150 <u>dwindled</u> from maybe fifty to a dozen. I was one of them. I'd made it to the last dozen. I knew this part of the tournament would take a while, because the guys who had lasted this long were good—they wouldn't easily fall into simple traps like the old lift-and-dive, 155 Hassan's favorite trick.

By three o'clock that afternoon, tufts of clouds had drifted in and the sun had slipped behind them. Shadows started to lengthen. The spectators on the roofs bundled up in scarves and thick coats. We were 160 down to a half dozen and I was still flying. My legs ached and my neck was stiff. But with each defeated kite, hope grew in my heart.

My eyes kept returning to a blue kite that had been <u>wreaking havoc</u> for the last hour.
165 "How many has he cut?" I asked.
"I counted eleven," Hassan said.
"Do you know whose it might be?"
Hassan clucked his tongue and tipped his chin. That was a trademark Hassan gesture, meant he had 170 no idea. The blue kite sliced a purple one and swept twice in big loops. Ten minutes later, he'd cut another two, sending <u>hordes</u> of kite runners racing after them.

After another thirty minutes, only four kites remained. And I was still flying. It seemed I could 175 hardly make a wrong move, as if every gust of wind blew in my favor. I'd never felt so in command, so lucky. It felt <u>intoxicating</u>. I <u>didn't dare</u> look up to the roof. Didn't dare take my eyes off the sky. I had to concentrate, play it smart. Another fifteen minutes

stealing glances: secretly looking

your mind drifted: it was difficult to concentrate

wandering: moving

surviving: remaining
dwindled: decreased

wreaking havoc: causing destruction

hordes: large groups

intoxicating: joyous; exciting
didn't dare: was afraid to

180 and what had seemed like a laughable dream that morning had suddenly become reality: It was just me and the other guy. The blue kite.

The tension in the air was as <u>taut</u> as the glass string I was tugging with my bloody hands. People
185 were stomping their feet, clapping, whistling, chanting, *"Boboresh! Boboresh!"* Cut him! Cut him! I wondered if Baba's voice was one of them. Music blasted. The smell of steamed *mantu* and fried *pakora* drifted from rooftops and open doors.

190 But all I heard—all I willed myself to hear—was the thudding of blood in my head. All I saw was the blue kite. All I smelled was victory. <u>Salvation</u>. <u>Redemption</u>. If Baba was wrong and there was a God like they said in school, then He'd let me win. I didn't know what the
195 other guy was playing for, maybe just <u>bragging rights</u>. But this was my one chance to become someone who was looked at, not seen, listened to, not heard. If
200 there was a God, He'd guide the winds, let them blow for me so that, with a tug of my string, I'd cut loose my pain, my longing. I'd endured too
205 much, come too far. And suddenly, just like that, hope became knowledge. I was going to win. It was just a matter of when.

210 It turned out to be sooner than later. A gust of wind lifted my kite and I took advantage. <u>Fed the string</u>, pulled up. Looped my kite on top of the blue one. I held position. The blue kite knew it was in trouble. It was trying desperately to <u>maneuver out of the jam</u>,
215 but I didn't let go. I held position. The crowd sensed the end was at hand. The chorus of "Cut him! Cut him!" grew louder, like <u>Romans chanting for the gladiators</u> to kill, kill!

"You're almost there, Amir agha! Almost there!"
220 Hassan was panting.

Then the moment came. I closed my eyes and loosened my grip on the string. It sliced my fingers again as the wind dragged it. And then. . . I didn't need to hear the <u>crowd's roar</u> to know. I didn't need to

taut: tight

salvation: the source of being saved from destruction

redemption: the act of freeing or restoring someone

bragging rights: permission to boast or say positive things about yourself

fed the string: released more string to enable the kite to rise

maneuver out of a jam: move to get out of trouble

Romans chanting for the gladiators: an ancient Roman custom of cheering for soldiers fighting lions

crowd's roar: the cheers of the people watching

142   Unit 7

225 see either. Hassan was screaming and his arm was wrapped around my neck.

"Bravo! Bravo, Amir agha!"

I opened my eyes, saw the blue kite spinning wildly like a tire come loose from a speeding car. I blinked,
230 tried to say something. Nothing came out.

Then I was screaming, and everything was color and sound, everything was alive and good. I was throwing my free arm around Hassan and we were hopping up and down, both of us laughing, both of us
235 weeping. "You won, Amir agha! You won!"

weeping: crying

"*We* won! *We* won!" was all I could say. This wasn't happening. In a moment, I'd blink and rouse from this beautiful dream, get out of bed, march down to the kitchen to eat breakfast with no one to talk to
240 but Hassan. Get dressed. Wait for Baba. Give up. Back to my old life. Then I saw Baba on our roof. He was standing on the edge, pumping both of his fists. Hollering and clapping. And that right there was the single greatest moment of my twelve years of life,
245 seeing Baba on the roof, proud of me at last.

But he was doing something now, motioning with his hands in an urgent way. Then I understood. "Hassan, we—"

"I know," he said, breaking our embrace. "*Inshallah*,
250 we'll celebrate later. Right now, I'm going to run that blue kite for you," he said. He dropped the spool and took off running, the hem of his green *chapan* dragging in the snow behind him.

Inshallah: God willing

"Hassan!" I called. "Come back with it!"
255 He was already turning the street corner, his rubber boots kicking up snow. He stopped, turned. He cupped his hands around his mouth. "For you a thousand times over!" he said. Then he smiled his Hassan smile and disappeared around the corner. The next time I saw
260 him smile unabashedly like that was twenty-six years later, in a faded Polaroid photograph.

unabashedly: without embarrassment

I hurried back to the street. I didn't want to see Baba yet. In my head, I had it all planned: I'd make a grand entrance, a hero, prized trophy in my bloodied hands.
265 Heads would turn and eyes would lock. A dramatic moment of silence. Then the old warrior would walk to the young one, embrace him, acknowledge his worthiness. Vindication. Salvation. Redemption. And then? Well . . . happily ever after, of course. What else?

eyes would lock: people would stare

acknowledge: admit the truth of
vindication: clearing one of blame

A. Summarizing the Story

IN ORDER TO SUMMARIZE THE MAIN IDEAS OF THE STORY, ASK YOURSELF:

- Who or what is this story about?
- What is the author trying to tell you about the relationships between the characters in the story?
- What actions in the story are most important?
- What does the action reveal about the characters?
- Does the action teach a lesson?

If someone asked you what The Kite Runner *was about, what would you say? In your notebook, write a paragraph that summarizes the main ideas of* The Kite Runner. *Use the questions in the box above to help you. Then share your summary with a partner.*

B. Understanding the Story

1. Building Tension

In the last excerpt of the story, the author continues the story of a kite contest. The narrative slowly builds to a climax with descriptions of the passing of time and of the number of kites still in the air.

Use numbers to put the sentences in the order in which they occur in the story.

___1___ Hassan licked his finger and held it up, tested the wind, then ran in its direction . . . . Within a minute, my kite was rocketing to the sky.

___5___ After another thirty minutes, only four kites remained. And I was still flying.

___6___ Another fifteen minutes and what had seemed like a laughable dream that morning had suddenly become a reality: It was just me and the other guy.

___4___ By three o'clock that afternoon . . . we were down to a half dozen and I was still flying.

___2___ Soon, the cutting started and the first of the defeated kites whirled out of control.

___3___ Within another hour, the number of surviving kites dwindled from maybe fifty to a dozen. I was one of them.

With a partner, read the sentences above in the correct order. Discuss how the writer builds tension. What other devices could a writer use to build tension?

2. Analyzing Descriptive Language

In The Kite Runner, *the author draws the reader into the action by appealing to all of the five senses, especially the senses of hearing, seeing, and smelling. In the box, write examples from the excerpts that appeal to these senses.*

Sense	Example from Text
Hearing	
Seeing	
Smelling	
Tasting	
Touching	

3. Making Inferences

Write answers to the following questions. Then share your answers with a partner.

1. What do you think the author is trying to say in the following sentences?

    a. " . . . this was my one chance to become someone who was looked at, not seen, listened to, not heard."

    _____

    b. " . . . with a tug of my string, I'd cut loose my pain, my longing. I'd endured too much, come too far."

    _____

    c. "And suddenly, just like that, hope became knowledge. I was going to win."

    _____

    d. "All I smelled was victory. Salvation. Redemption."

    _____

2. How do Amir and Hassan feel about each other at the end of the contest? What do you think happens to their relationship? Which lines support your opinions?

    _____

    _____

    _____

3. After he wins, Amir pictures the scene with his father. What does he think will happen when he sees his father? Will they live "happily ever after"?

    _____

    _____

    _____

4. Point-of-View Writing

The Kite Runner is narrated by Amir. This story would be different if it were told from another character's point of view. Write a letter in which you describe the kite contest from the point of view of Hassan, Amir's servant, or Baba, Amir's father.

C. Working with Language

Complete the story of another contest, a spelling bee, with the words and phrases below. Use the synonyms in parentheses under the blanks to help you choose the best answer.

didn't dare	**glared**	**pack it in**
dwindled	**huddled**	**putting myself through this**
gaze	**an open book**	**stole a glance**

It was our annual spelling bee—the boys against the girls. The number of students on the stage had _____1_____ (decreased) from twelve to just four. I was the only girl left standing on the stage. Dressed in my white blouse, green school jumper, and green lace-up shoes, I stood awkwardly on the stage as the boys _____2_____ (stared angrily) at me and willed me to make a mistake. I wanted to _____3_____ (quit, give up). Who cared if the boys won? I certainly didn't. Why was I _____4_____ (forcing myself to do)? I peeled my gaze away from the girls who stood _____5_____ (gathered together) in small groups in the back of the room. Instead, I _____6_____ (secretly looked) at the boy I secretly admired. My mind drifted. What would he think of me if I won? All of the boys would hate me even more.

I _____7_____ (was afraid to) let anyone know what I was thinking. I had to be careful. My mother called me _____8_____ (a person who can't hide feelings); it was easy to figure out what I was thinking by looking at my face. I snapped my _____9_____ (look; attention) back to the announcer as he suddenly called my name. There were two of us on the stage now—just Tommy Ford and me. "Your word is 'guarantee'. Can you spell 'guarantee'?"

Can I? Should I? I wondered.

"Guarantee" I repeated, "g-a-u-r-a-n-t-e-e."

D. Open for Discussion

Discuss these questions in a small group. Then choose one question and summarize the group's discussion of it in your notebook.

1. In what ways is the spelling bee, in the exercise on page 147, like the kite flying competition from *The Kite Runner*? How are they different? Why is success important for each of the characters? What does their success represent in each case?

2. What does reading literature from other cultures teach us? Can we truly learn about another culture from fiction? In what other ways can we learn about a culture?

3. Do sons generally feel a need to impress their fathers? Is this true for you or the sons and fathers that you know? Is it the same for fathers and daughters? Mothers and daughters? Mothers and sons? If not, why not? How is the father–son relationship different from other parent–child relationships?

4. Can true friends come from different classes of society or different cultures? Do factors like class and culture make a difference to childhood friends? At what point in a child's life do they start to matter? Why?

5. Do you think our dreams can teach us something about ourselves? Did a dream ever help you understand something that was happening in real life? If so, how? What are some common images in dreams? What do you think they might represent?

6. Why do you think the word *dream* is used in many languages both for the images you experience while sleeping and for the wishes you have for your future? How does this second type of dream—wishes for your future—affect your life? Do you consider dreams to be fantasies, or are they goals that people should try to achieve?

IV Structured Writing Focus

YOUR TASK

Write a five-paragraph essay in which you analyze one aspect of *The Kite Runner*. Describe the relationship between Amir and his father OR Amir and his friend, Hassan. Discuss how the figurative language in the excerpt helps to reveal the nature of the relationships. Be sure to support your opinions with examples from the story. Use line numbers to refer to your examples.

ALTERNATIVE TASK: **Discuss how the author uses symbolism. Who or what does the kite symbolize? Who or what does the monster in the lake symbolize? What does the kite contest symbolize? Can you find any other symbols?**

A. Starting to Write

1. Brainstorming

Follow the directions for each task. Then, in your notebook, write notes for your essay on the questions.

FOR THE MAIN TASK

Amir and his father
Go back to the story excerpts and underline all the sentences that refer to Amir's father. Notice that Amir's father never speaks in these excerpts, yet the reader gets a clear impression of Amir's relationship with his father. Based on these sentences, what do you think? Does Amir love his father? Does his father love him? Why is Amir happy he won the kite contest? What does he hope will happen as a result? How does Hassan seem to come between Amir and his father?

Amir and Hassan
Go back to the story excerpts and underline all the sentences that refer to Hassan. In Afghanistan at this time it was typical for a wealthy, young boy to have servants. In what ways does Hassan serve Amir? How does Amir feel about Hassan? How does Hassan feel about Amir? How do you think the class difference between the two affects their relationship? What do you think will happen to their relationship in the future?

In literature, authors often use **symbols** in a narrative to convey a message. This allows a story to be interpreted in several ways. For example, on a realistic level, this story is about a boy flying his kite in a contest and his excitement at winning. On a deeper, more symbolic level, the kite might be a symbol for Amir and his feelings. The major symbolism in this story is the kite contest, which is portrayed as a battle or an initiation.

Think about the symbols of the kite, the monster in the lake, and the kite contest. Answer the questions below. Then find a line reference in the reading to support your answer. Write the quote in the box and then explain it. After you complete your charts, use them to help you organize and support your opinions.

1. What could the **kite** symbolize? Select three choices that make sense to you.
   a. Amir's emotions at the start of the contest
   b. the relationship between Hassan and Amir
   c. a weapon used to defeat your enemy
   d. the pain a person experiences in a battle
   e. hope

Symbolism	Quote	Explanation
a. Amir's emotions at the start of the contest	The kite rocketing into the sky (lines 108–109)	Amir has overcome his fears & is excited at the start of the contest.

2. What could the **monster in the lake** symbolize? Select three choices that make sense to you.
   a. Amir's fear of failure
   b. Amir's fear of his father
   c. Amir's dream of fulfillment
   d. Amir's view of himself
   e. Amir's burden to prove himself

Symbolism	Reference	Explanation

3. What could the **kite contest** symbolize? Select three choices that make sense to you.
   a. Amir's desire to prove himself to himself
   b. Amir's desire to prove himself to his father
   c. Amir's desire to show his intelligence
   d. the social positions of Amir and Hassan
   e. Hassan's importance in Amir's life

Symbolism	Reference	Explanation

B. Preparing the First Draft

1. Introducing a Literary Analysis Essay

An introduction to this kind of essay varies somewhat from other essay introductions. A hook always adds interest, but it is optional. However, it is very important to include:

- The title* and author of the literary text you are analyzing

- Information that identifies the characters in the text

- A two- to three-sentence summary of the text and/or general statements that relate to the text

- A thesis statement that reflects your opinion and essay organization

Compare these two introductions to essays on The Kite Runner. *In a small group, discuss the questions that follow.*

ORIGINAL INTRODUCTION

> The process of becoming a real adult has always been a complex one, and the father–son conflict is one of its most important components. Since Biblical times, sons have always been trying to defy their fathers, but at the same time, they have looked for their love and acknowledgement. The relationship between Amir and his father is a good example of how difficult it can be for a child to manage with a silent and authoritative father.

REVISED INTRODUCTION

> "And that right there was the single greatest moment of my twelve years of life, seeing Baba on the roof, proud of me at last" (243–245). That is how Amir, a young Afghan boy in Khaled Hosseini's novel The Kite Runner, felt when he won the kite contest. His father, Baba, would be "proud of [him] at last," and they would "live happily ever after" (269). As Hosseini shows in his novel, the process of becoming an adult has always been a complex one, and the father–son conflict is one of the most important components of this process. Since Biblical times, sons have tried to defy their fathers, but at the same time, they have longed for their love and acknowledgement. The strained relationship between Amir and his father in The Kite Runner is a good example of how difficult it can be for a child to grow up with a silent and authoritative father.

---

* Note: Remember to italicize or underline the title of a book. Use quotation marks when discussing a short story or chapter from a book. See Unit 4 for more on citations.

1. What did the author use as a hook in his revised essay? What else could have been used?

2. Do the author's general statements relate to the topic?

3. What information did the author add to the thesis statement? Why?

4. What else did the author change? Why?

2. Using Quotes from the Text as Support

Quotes are specific lines from a text, set off by quotation marks. In the body of a literary analysis essay, support for your thesis will consist of your own opinions. To strengthen this support, include quotes from the piece that you are analyzing.

The best way to include quotes in an essay is to "sandwich" the quotes between explanations:

- introduce the quote by indicating where it occurs in the action of the text and who said it or who it applies to

- add the quote

- end with an explanation of the quote in your own words

Look at this example*:

Introduction to quote → Amir also loved his friend, Hassan. When Amir's kite cut the blue

Direct quote → kite, the last one, Amir shouted, "We won! We won!" (236). Clearly,

Explanation of quote → Amir feels that he would not have won without Hassan's help.

When you are using several quotes in a paragraph and it is obvious who is speaking, you can vary your use of quotes by beginning with an explanation and then adding the quote.

Compare the two body paragraphs for an essay on The Kite Runner. *Discuss the questions that follow in small groups or with a partner.*

ORIGINAL BODY PARAGRAPH

For Amir, his father is both an absent and always present figure. Amir seems to be immersed in a struggle to get some feedback from this almost divine person. As is usual in any unequal relationship, the result is both frustrating and distressing. All of us, like Amir, have looked for our moment of glory in front of our fathers, after which everything is going to be right with ourselves and the world around us.

REVISED BODY PARAGRAPH

For Amir, his father is both an absent and always present figure. In the first excerpt, Amir says, "Upstairs, I could hear the water running in Baba's bathroom" (36). Just before the contest, he says, "Baba was on the roof, watching me" (64). Amir seems to be immersed in a struggle to get some positive feedback from this almost divine person who is always there, but never says a word to him. As is usual in any unequal relationship, the result is both frustrating and distressing. During the contest Amir says, "I kept stealing glances at Baba sitting on the roof, wondered what he was thinking. Was he cheering for me? Or did a part of him want to see me fail?" (135–137). Amir is never sure what his father thinks of him; most of the time he assumes his father disapproves of him. All of us, like Amir, have looked for our moment of glory in front of our fathers, after which everything is going to be right with ourselves and the world around us: "In my head, I had it all planned: I'd make a grand entrance, a hero, prized trophy in my bloodied hands" (263–264).

1. How many quotes does the writer use? Do the quotes help to support the writer's opinions? How?

2. Which quotes does the writer sandwich between an introduction and an explanation? Look closely at the last quote in the revised paragraph. How is it different from the other quotes in this paragraph?

3. How does the writer punctuate the quotes? How does the punctuation differ between a quote that is a statement and one that is a question?

Note: Give page numbers if your quote is from a book. Use line numbers if your quote is from a book excerpt, a short story, or a poem. Place the numbers inside parentheses ( ). See Unit 4 for more on citations.

3. Understanding Figurative Language

Figurative language is often used in writing to illuminate themes in fiction. In *The Kite Runner*, **similes**, **metaphors**, and **personification** are used to clarify the nature of the relationship between Amir and Hassan, the relationship between Amir and his father, the atmosphere on the day of the contest, and Hassan's feelings in response to what is taking place.

Similes and metaphors both show the similarity between two essentially unlike things or concepts.

SIMILE

Similes contain the word "as'" or "like" and are therefore explicit comparisons.

It was warm and sunny, and <u>the lake</u> was clear **like a mirror**.

Comparing the clearness of the lake to a mirror suggests to the reader that the lake is a reflection of something—in this case, Amir.

<u>The father's gaze</u> was **as hard and cold as steel**.

Here the hardness and coldness of steel is a simile for the nature of the father's gaze. It helps the reader understand that Amir's father is not a warm, loving man. It can also suggest to the reader that Amir is afraid of his father.

METAPHOR

Metaphors apply a word or phrase that designates one thing to another thing in an implicit comparison.

<u>The challenge</u> that confronted him was **a fifty-foot wall**.

Here the 50-foot wall is a metaphor for a difficult challenge. The reader understands that the challenge is something almost impossible to overcome.

Note: A *symbol* and a *metaphor* are similar. A metaphor, however, is more of a comparison. It focuses on what is alike between the objects being compared. A symbol is an object that stands for something else and may originally have little in common with the object it is representing, such as the stars on the United States flag representing the states in the United States.

PERSONIFICATION

Personification uses human qualities or form to represent abstractions or inanimate objects.

But with each **defeated kite**, hope grew in my heart. . . .

Here the author describes the kite as "defeated," an adjective that is used with people, such as "defeated soldiers." This attaches human emotion to the kite, emotion that the reader can understand and relate to. It also suggests that the kite contest is some sort of battle.

Look back at the excerpts from The Kite Runner *in this unit. Find examples of figurative language and write them below. Indicate in each case whether the example is a simile (S), a metaphor (M), or personification (P). Compare your answers with a partner and briefly discuss what each one illustrates. Put an asterisk (*) next to the ones that lend support to the specific writing task you are working on.*

4. Organizing Your Essay

Study these block diagrams to help you write your essay on the main task or the alternative task. In your notebook, draw your own diagram and write your notes in each of its sections.

INTRODUCTION
Hook
Title, author's name, and character identification
Summary and/or general statements
Thesis Statement

MAIN TASK

BODY ¶ 1
Point 1 about the relationship
Support with examples and quotes from the text
Relevant personal examples (optional)

BODY ¶ 2
Point 2 about the relationship
Support with examples and quotes from the text
Relevant personal examples (optional)

BODY ¶ 3
Point 3 about the relationship
Support with examples and quotes from the text
Relevant personal examples (optional)

ALTERNATIVE TASK

BODY ¶ 1
Introduce symbol 1 and its meaning
Support with examples and quotes from the text

BODY ¶ 2
Introduce symbol 2 and its meaning
Support with examples and quotes from the text

BODY ¶ 3
Introduce symbol 3 and its meaning
Support with examples and quotes from the text

CONCLUSION
Restatement of your thesis
Summary of main points
Something to think about
Include key words and phrases to unify your essay

*Write a **first draft** of your essay. Remember to write in complete sentences and try to use some of the vocabulary and structures that you have practiced in this unit.*

C. Revising the First Draft

When you have finished writing your first draft, read it to a partner.

CHECKLIST FOR REVISING THE FIRST DRAFT

When you listen to your partner's essay and when you discuss your own, keep these questions in mind:

1. Are the title, author, and characters from the text identified in the introduction?

2. Does the thesis statement answer the question implicit in the assignment?

3. Does each body paragraph have a clear topic sentence?

4. Does the support include examples and quotes from the text?

5. Are the quotes punctuated correctly? Are line numbers included?

6. How did the writer unify this essay? Is the thesis restated in the conclusion?

After discussing your essay with a partner, you may want to add, change, or omit some information.

*Now write a **second draft** that includes all of your additions and changes.*

D. Editing the Second Draft

After you have written a second draft, proofread your work for any errors and correct them. These guidelines and exercises should help.

Use of Unreal Conditionals in Literary Analysis

In general, we use the present tense to discuss literature:

When Amir wins the contest, he looks up and sees his father cheering for him.

You can also use the past tense:

When Amir won the contest, he looked up and saw his father cheering for him.

Whichever tense you choose, you must use it consistently.

When discussing how things in a story might be different in the present or might have been different in the past, use **unreal conditionals**. Using conditionals in this way helps you and your reader better understand the behavior and motivations of characters in literature. **You must be consistent with conditionals also**. If you are using present tense in your discussion of the story, use **present unreal conditional**. If you are using past tense, use **past unreal conditional**.

Present Unreal Conditional
if + simple past . . . conditional (*would / might* + base form)

If Amir and Hassan **weren't** so close in age, their relationship **might be** different.

Past Unreal Conditional
if + past perfect . . . conditional (*would / might* + have + past participle)

If Amir and Hassan **hadn't been** so close in age, their relationship **might have been** different.

Answer these questions using the appropriate conditional form.

1. How might their relationship be different if Amir and Hassan weren't so close in age?

   Amir might _____

   Hassan might not _____

2. In his dream about the monster, Hassan jumps into the water after Amir and starts swimming. In real life, Hassan can't swim.

   If he hadn't been dreaming, Hassan _____.

Combine these sentences using either the present or past unreal conditional form. Compare your sentences with a partner.

1. a. Amir didn't sleep well the night before the kite-running contest.

   b. The morning before the contest, Amir was mean to Hassan.

   _____

   _____

2. a. Hassan understands Amir better than Amir understands himself.

   b. Amir doesn't need to apologize to Hassan for being mean.

   _____

   _____

3. Amir knew that winning the contest would help him gain approval from his father.

   a. Amir wanted very much to gain his father's approval.

   b. Amir was extremely nervous before the kite contest.

   _____

   _____

4. On the morning of the contest, Amir's courage wavers, and he nearly decides not to enter the contest.

   a. Hassan tells Amir his dream about the monster in the lake.

   b. This gives Amir the courage to enter the contest.

   _____

   _____

5. a. Amir isn't close to his father.

   b. Amir wonders whether his father wants him to fail in the kite contest.

   _____

   _____

E. Preparing the Final Draft

Reread your second draft and correct any errors you find. Put a check (✓) in each space as you edit for these points. Then write your corrected final version.

CHECKLIST FOR EDITING THE SECOND DRAFT

_____ consistent use of tense when discussing literature

_____ use of unreal conditionals in a literary analysis essay

 ## V Additional Writing Opportunities

1. They say a servant knows his master better than the master knows his servant. Do you think this is true? Why or why not? Does it only apply to traditional master-and-servant relationships, or can it be broadened to other unequal relationships? Defend your answer using examples from *The Kite Runner,* other books or stories you have read, or movies or television programs you have seen.

2. Analyze a famous literary friendship between unequals. For example, Tom Sawyer and Huckleberry Finn in *The Adventures of Huckleberry Finn;* Sherlock Holmes and Doctor Watson in any of A.C. Doyle's novels about the great detective; Reuven Malder and Danny Sanders in Chaim Potok's *The Chosen.* Analyze the friendship in terms of what the friends do for each other and the benefit each derives from the relationship. Draw a conclusion about how strong the friendship is in light of the differences between the two people.

3. Analyze the relationship between a father and son in a well-known book, story, or film. You might consider the relationship between Willy Loman and Happy or Biff in Arthur Miller's play, "Death of a Salesman," or between Bull and Ben Meechum in Pat Conroy's novel, *The Great Santini.* In examining the relationship, consider what the two say to each other and about each other, what they do or don't do for each other, and how others characterize their relationship.

4. Discuss the author's use of description in *The Kite Runner.* How do his descriptions add to the excitement of the contest? How do they reveal the relationship between Amir and his father? How do they express Amir's conflicting feelings about Hassan? Find as many examples from the story as possible to convince your readers.

5. What role should competition play in a child's life? Think about a competition or contest you have participated in. Were the participants encouraged to be as competitive as possible or to cooperate with one another? Is this different for boys and girls? Is being competitive something that we should encourage in children?

WRITING AN ARGUMENTATIVE ESSAY

In this unit you will practice:
- identifying arguments and counterarguments
- refuting an argument
- organizing an argumentative essay
- synthesizing information to form arguments

Editing focus:
- unstated conditionals
- noun clauses

I Fluency Practice: Freewriting

Is there a difference between an unethical act and an illegal one? Think about downloading[1] movies and music without paying. In most cases that is illegal. But is it also unethical?

Write for ten minutes. Try to express yourself as well as you can. Don't worry about mistakes. Share your writing with your partner.

---

download: to take material off the Internet and put it on your own computer

163

Reading for Writing

This reading is adapted from a *New York Times* article about the response by the Pennsylvania State University to students who violate copyright laws by downloading music from the Internet without paying.

STUDENTS SHALL NOT DOWNLOAD. YEAH, SURE.

By Kate Zernike

In the rough and tumble of the student union here at Pennsylvania State University (Penn State), the moral code is purely pragmatic.

Thou shalt[1] not smoke—it will kill you.

Thou shalt not take a term paper off the Internet—it will get you kicked out.[2]

5 Thou shalt not use a fake ID—it will get you arrested.

And when it comes to downloading music or movies off the Internet, students here compare it with under-age drinking: illegal, but not immoral. Like alcohol and parties, the Internet is easily accessible. Why not download, or drink, when "everyone" does it?

10 This set of commandments[3] has helped make people between the ages of 18 and 29, and college students in particular, the biggest downloaders of Internet music.

15 "It's not something you feel guilty about doing," said Dan Langlitz, 20, a junior here. "You don't get the feeling it's illegal because it's so easy." He held an MP3 player[4] in his hand.

20 "They sell these things, the sites are there. Why is it illegal?"

Students say they have had the Internet for as long as they can remember, and have grown up

25 thinking of it as theirs for the taking. The array of services available to them on campus has only encouraged that sense. Penn State recently made the student center, known as the Hub, entirely wireless, so students do not even have to

30 dial up to get on the Internet. Many course materials—textbook excerpts, articles, syllabi—are online. Residence halls offer fast broadband

---

1. *thou shalt:* you should (old-fashioned; currently used only in religious contexts)
2. *get kicked out:* be forced to leave
3. *commandments:* important rules of behavior, originally from the Bible
4. *MP3 player:* a device for downloading and playing music from the Internet

access—which studies say makes people more likely to download.

Last year and again last week, the university sent out an e-mail message reminding students that downloading copyrighted music is
35 illegal, and pleading with them to "resist the urge" to download. This year, all students had to take an online tutorial before receiving access to their e-mail accounts, acknowledging that they had read and agreed to university policy prohibiting the downloading of copyrighted material.

To students, the crackdown[5] seemed like a sudden reversal. "Up until
40 recently, we were not told it was wrong," said Kristin Ebert, 19. "We think if it's available, you can use it. It's another resource."

Penn State has taken a harder line than most other campuses. But whether here or at other campuses, students do not seem to be grasping the moral message. Ann Morrissey, 19, confessed that she had not even listened
45 to all the songs she had downloaded. "I have 400 songs, I listen to 20," she said. "I don't know why," she added, then laughed self-consciously, and answered herself, "You can, and it's cool to have them." She, like others, does not see the harm done, and remains suspicious of the recording industry.

The university has sent warnings to a couple of hundred students. But
50 on a campus with 42,000 students, punishment seems remote to many. "No one close to home has gotten in trouble," said Andrew Ricken, a junior. A common analogy—downloading music is like stealing a CD— does not sway students.

At best, the new warnings seemed to have some students negotiating
55 new rules. At a table with friends, John Dixon was debating whether he would be caught if he traded songs only with his roommates on their local area network, off campus. Just to be safe, he is sticking mostly to downloading music from CDs. He is not sharing his files—not because he sees it as illegal, but because he hears that the record industry is going
60 mainly after sharers, not downloaders.

Ms. Wilson, too, is not sharing, though she has continued downloading. "That doesn't make it right," she said. "But it's not that big a deal, right?"

---

5. *crackdown:* sudden disciplinary action

A. General Understanding

1. What Do You Think?

Use the information in the reading to help you form opinions on the topic of downloading. Answer these questions in your notebook. Then share your answers with a partner.

1. What is the university's position on downloading? What is it doing to discourage downloading? What else would you advise the administration of Penn State to do?

2. How have students at Penn State responded to the university's tough policy on downloading? Does the university indirectly encourage students to download? How?

3. In your experience, do student "commandments" like those at Pennsylvania State University exist at other schools? What are some other possible commandments? How do you feel about the commandment not to download music or movies without paying?

2. Identifying Arguments and Counterarguments

As additional evidence that students don't consider music piracy wrong, the author uses a number of quotes by various students at Penn State.

Read the arguments the students make. Then, with a partner, discuss whether each argument is a strong one or a weak one and decide on a counterargument. Add your own argument in the last box.

Student Argument	Counterargument
from the article: "Why not download, or drink, when 'everyone' does it."	This is a weak argument for several reasons. First of all, not everyone does it. Second, even the action of a majority of people can be wrong.

Student Argument	Counterargument
Dan Langlitz, 20: "They sell these things (MP3 players). The sites are there. Why is it illegal?"	
Kristen Ebert, 19: "Up until recently, we were not told it was wrong."	
Ann Morrissey, 19: "I have 400 songs. I listen to 20... it's cool to have them."	
Andrew Ricken, a junior: "No one close to home has gotten in trouble."	
Other argument:	

B. Working with Language

1. Using Context Clues

Match the words with their definitions. Then read the sentences that follow and use the context to help you choose the best word to complete each sentence.

_____ 1. copyright   a. an impulse toward; a desire

_____ 2. monitor   b. too much, too great

_____ 3. grasping   c. relating to practical affairs

_____ 4. pragmatic   d. the exclusive legal right to an artistic work

_____ 5. urge   e. fully understanding

_____ 6. excessive   f. watch or check for a particular purpose

1. Students at Penn State have been punished for _____ downloading. Now, they are allowed to download only a certain amount.

2. University officials are not concerned with the ethics of downloading music without paying. They are concerned with _____ issues, such as whether the university will be held responsible for the illegal activity.

3. The record industry has taken over two hundred people to court for sharing music files in violation of _____ laws.

4. Despite the fact that some people have been fined $12,000 dollars for sharing music files, students are having a hard time _____ the moral message that downloading is wrong.

5. For some students, the fear of fines is enough. They have stopped downloading because they worry that record companies will hack into their systems and _____ their activities online.

6. For some, however, the _____ to download their favorite music at no cost is too strong to resist. They will continue to download and hope not to get caught.

2. Idioms in Context

Here are four idioms that use or incorporate the word "line." Read the sentences and then write the correct idiom next to the definition in the box.

Penn State **has taken a harder line** than most other campuses. It denies students access to the Internet if they share music files.

The ease of **going online** has shaped not only attitudes about downloading, but cheating as well, **blurring the lines** between right and wrong.

Music companies say that a lot of people don't know where **to draw the line** when it comes to getting music off the Internet.

Definition	Idiom
1. to stop an action	
2. adopted a strict policy	
3. connecting to the Internet	
4. causing more confusion	

3. Using Vocabulary on Your Own

What do you think about downloading music and movies from the Internet without paying ? Using some of the vocabulary you have learned in this section, write a paragraph in which you give your opinion and explain your reasons.

_____

_____

_____

_____

_____

_____

_____

_____

III Prewriting Activities

A. Theories of Ethics

1. Synthesizing Information

Ethics is the study of right and wrong. Philosophers Immanuel Kant, John Stuart Mill, and Aristotle all developed theories of ethics. Dr. Joseph Chuman, leader of the Bergen Ethical Culture Society, summarized their philosophies as follows. Read the summaries and answer the questions that follow in your notebooks. Share your answers with a partner.

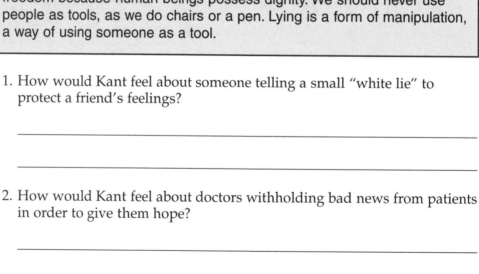

IMMANUEL KANT

Immanuel Kant proposed that when you make a moral decision, you should ask yourself a question: What if everyone acted this way? Kant advocated the use
5 of maxims, personal rules that you use to make a moral decision. He said that you must never act in a way that contradicts a maxim. For Kant, there is no concept of "sometimes." He was an absolutist.
10 One of Kant's maxims is that we must never lie. He once said that he would tell a murderer where his intended victim was hiding. Because we cannot predict consequences, we must ignore them and be consistent.
15 According to Kant, people must respect all other people and their freedom because human beings possess dignity. We should never use people as tools, as we do chairs or a pen. Lying is a form of manipulation, a way of using someone as a tool.

1. How would Kant feel about someone telling a small "white lie" to protect a friend's feelings?

_____

_____

2. How would Kant feel about doctors withholding bad news from patients in order to give them hope?

_____

_____

JOHN STUART MILL

John Stuart Mill believed that if you
20 want to act morally, you have to look at
consequences. He said that you must
use your imagination and try to predict
the results of your actions. For Mill, you
are acting morally if the consequences
25 of your action bring happiness to the
greatest number of people, including
yourself. If people will suffer because of
your action, then you shouldn't do it.
   Because Mill's ideas only deal with
30 consequences, his philosophy of ethics is called utilitarianism. In Mill's
view, you should weigh the morality of an action in terms of its utility,
or usefulness.

1. You are walking on the beach and you see someone in the water
   drowning. According to Mill, what should you do?

2. What would Mill's position be on testing experimental drugs on people
   who are terminally ill?

ARISTOTLE

For Aristotle, those things that help us grow and flourish are good, and
35 those things that stifle or stunt our growth are bad. Aristotle's concept of growth includes those physical and social things that are necessary for human development. The physical
40 things include clean air and water and good food. The social things include friendship, supportive social relationships, and education.

If you are attempting to live an
45 ethical life, Aristotle said you should ask yourself what kind of person you want to become. Then you can make moral choices based on whether an action will help you become that person.

1. What would Aristotle have thought about someone who prefers the company of his computer to that of other human beings?

_____

_____

_____

_____

2. What might Aristotle have said to someone who stole medicine from another sick person because he could not afford to buy it?

_____

_____

_____

_____

2. Comparing Kant, Mill, and Aristotle

What do you think Kant, Mill, and Aristotle would think about downloading music and movies from the Internet without paying? Look again at the passages on pages 170-172. In the following chart, indicate whether each philosopher would consider it ethical or unethical and explain why.

	Ethical: Yes or No?	Why?
Kant		
Mill		
Aristotle		

Which philosopher(s) do you agree with? How strongly? Do their theories reinforce your initial reaction to the issue of downloading or do they make you reconsider your point of view? Write a paragraph in response to these questions and share it with a partner.

3. Open for Discussion

Discuss these questions in a small group. Then choose one of the questions and write a summary of the group's discussion about it in your notebook.

1. What criteria or standards do you use when deciding if something is right or wrong? Give an example of a time when you had to choose between two alternatives and had a difficult time deciding what was right.

2. Do you think your ideas of what is right and wrong are different from those of people of your parents' generation? Your grandparents' generation? How are they different? How would you explain the change in people's thinking?

3. Does your school have a policy on cheating? What would you do if you saw someone violating it?

Ⅳ Structured Writing Focus

YOUR TASK

Write a five-paragraph argumentative essay about the ethics of downloading music from the Internet without paying. Use information from the reading and from the three theories of ethics to help you form your opinion.

ALTERNATIVE TASK: Write a five-paragraph argumentative essay on the ethics of refusing to provide life-saving medicines to anyone not able to pay full price. Use information from the reading and from the three theories of ethics to help you form your opinion.

A. Starting to Write

Brainstorming

FOR THE MAIN TASK

Look back at the chart you prepared on page 173. Reread the paragraph you wrote about your own opinion. Make a list of what you feel are the best arguments to support your opinion. Be sure to indicate the source of the argument so you can cite it properly in your essay.

FOR THE ALTERNATIVE TASK

Read the following fictional dilemma, which social psychologist Lawrence Kohlberg presented to people as part of his research into moral development.

A woman was near death from a rare kind of cancer. There was one drug that doctors thought might save her—a form of radium that a druggist in the same town had recently discovered. The drug was expensive to make, but the druggist was charging ten times what the drug cost to produce. He paid $200 for the radium but charged $2,000 for the drug. The sick woman's husband, Heinz, went to everyone he knew to borrow the money, but he could only raise $1,000, half of what the drug cost. Heinz told the druggist that his wife was dying and asked him to sell it cheaper or let him pay later. But the druggist said, "No, I discovered the drug, and I am going to make money from it." Heinz became desperate. He broke into the man's store and stole the drug for his wife.

Talk about the dilemma in small groups. Include these questions in your discussion.

1. Should Heinz have broken into the druggist's store and stolen the drug?

2. Which of the philosophers would say that the husband had no choice but to steal the drug? Which would say that he should not, under any circumstances, steal the drug?

3. In matters of life and death, should all other considerations be given less weight?

4. Is there a right answer to this problem? Is it possible for a problem to have no ethical solution?

Look again at the passages on pages 170–172. In the chart, write what you think each philosopher would do in Heinz's situation and why. Then write what you would do and why.

	Action	Why?
Kant		
Mill		
Aristotle		
Myself		

B. Preparing the First Draft

1. Analyzing an Argumentative Essay

This model essay is written in an **argumentative essay** form. The writer presents her opinions and uses information from several sources to support those opinions.

The writer also examines the opposing arguments and explains why she disagrees with them. This is known as the **counterargument** and **refutation**. She includes a **concession** on points in the opposing argument that she sees as valid in Body Paragraph 2.

Read this essay about the ethics of the actions of a student named John. Then analyze each paragraph of the argumentative essay by filling in the blanks in the outlines. Some of the blanks have been filled in for you.

Is it wrong to hand in someone else's work as your own? Of course. Instinctively, we all know that it is. But often when faced with the decision of whether or not we should cheat, we overlook the morality of the situation, and do what seems best for us at that moment. John did just that. John was in his last semester of college. It was 12 a.m. and he was having trouble finishing the last question of a five-part essay exam in Linguistics. He knew that if he didn't hand it in on time, he would fail the course and not be able to graduate that semester. His friend, Carol, offered to write the answer for him. He let her do that section, and handed in Carol's work as his own. He passed the course, graduated, and went on to teach English in the public school system. Regardless of the outcome, however, when John decided to submit someone else's work as his own, he was wrong. Although ethicist John Stuart Mill might not agree with this verdict, philosophers Immanuel Kant and Aristotle would. With their support, the case against John's actions is made even stronger.

I. Introduction

    A. Hook: _____

    B. General statements:

        1. <u>instinctively, we know it's wrong</u> _____

        2. _____

        3. _____

    C. Thesis Statement: _____

Body Paragraph 1

The greatest wrong was done to John's professor. Submitting Carol's work as his own shows an extreme lack of respect for the professor. According to Dr. Joseph Chuman, Immanuel Kant would say, "Lying is a form of manipulation, a way of using someone as a tool" (17). Human beings should always be treated with respect because they "possess dignity." In fact, Kant feels it is wrong to lie under any circumstances. While my view is less black and white than this, I feel that John violated the trust of his professor and made a fool of him as well. Kant, as quoted in Chuman, would ask, "What if everyone acted this way?" (4) The answer would be that no one could trust anyone. John assumed his professor would fail him if he handed in his essay late, but he did not know this. His professor might have made an exception in this case, as John was so close to graduation. Kant's position is summarized as, "Because we cannot predict consequences, we must ignore them and be consistent" (13).

II. Body Paragraphs

A. Argument 1: John's lie showed a lack of respect for his professor.

1. Support 1: Kant's philosophy

   a. _____

   b. _humans possess dignity_____

   c. _____

   d. _____

2. Support 2: writer's interpretation of Kant

   a. _not as black and white_____

   b. _____

Body Paragraph 2

Some would argue that no one was truly hurt when John used Carol's answer; several people even benefited. Chuman maintains that philosopher John Stuart Mill would take this position. According to Chuman, Mill would say, "you are acting morally if the consequences of your action bring happiness to the greatest number of people, including yourself"(23). In this case, using Carol's answer "brought happiness" to both Carol and John. Carol was anxious to win John's approval; John was able to complete the course and graduate on time. In fact, John's future students were helped immeasurably by having a good English teacher. What benefit would have come from John's failing the course? Mill suggests that the consequences of an action should be evaluated according to the benefits that they bring. This makes sense because the consequences of failing to graduate would have been too harsh, as they would have affected John's whole future. Nevertheless, it is dangerous to accept a philosophy that encourages people to believe that the end justifies the means.

B. Counterargument: Several people benefited by John's action

Support: quote about consequences

a. _Carol got John's approval_

b. _____

c. _____

Concession: _the consequences would have been too harsh_

Refutation: _____

Body Paragraph 3

John's action, however, did hurt someone. It hurt John. By using Carol's answer, John did not learn to accept the consequences of his failure to complete the assignment. He never learned whether he could have answered that question on his own. He never had the satisfaction of receiving a grade based on his own work. Moreover, he will always look back on this incident with shame and regret. Chuman contends that Aristotle would tell John that using his friend's work is wrong. According to Chuman, Aristotle viewed actions that "stifle or stunt our growth" (35), such as failing to honestly do what's expected of us, as wrong. John hurt himself, which is obvious by his regret. His action made it harder for him to mature into a person he could respect.

C. Refutation/Argument 2: John was hurt, not helped, by using his friend's essay

Support 1: writer's opinions

a. _John did not learn to accept consequences_

b. _____

c. _____

d. _____

Support 2: writer's interpretation of Aristotle's views

a. _____

b. _____

Conclusion

Our instincts tell us John was wrong to submit Carol's work as his own, and our instincts are right. It was wrong for John to lie to his professor and manipulate him into grading Carol's answer. Perhaps Kant's position that people should never lie is too idealistic for our complex world, but his broader idea is still valid: it is wrong to undermine someone else's integrity in order to achieve our own personal goals. In addition, it was wrong for John to focus only on the consequences of not completing the assignment. This reflects Mill's idea that the ends justify the means. Though it is easy to argue that this is sometimes true, it can also put us in the position of being untrue to ourselves, as with John. Instead, John should have thought about the person he wanted to become, as Aristotle would advise him to do. How would he feel if one of *his* students handed in someone else's work?

III. Conclusion

A. Restatement of thesis: _____

_____

B. Key words repeated to unify essay:

instincts _____

_____

consequences _____

_____

C. Summary of main points:

1. _____

2. wrong to manipulate a person _____

3. _____

D. Concluding thoughts

1. advice: _____

2. something to think about: How would John feel if his

students lied to him? _____

180   Unit 8

2. Refuting an Argument

In order to convince the reader of your point of view, you must *refute* opposing arguments, showing that they are weak or incorrect.

Consider this situation: A university student has been accused of plagiarizing in her senior thesis. A faculty committee is reviewing her case and will decide whether she is guilty of plagiarism. If she is found guilty, she will not be allowed to graduate.

For each of the student's arguments below, write a possible refutation by the faculty committee in your notebook. Share your refutations with a partner.

Student's argument	Refutation by faculty committee
Plagiarizing means copying a large chunk of material from a single source. I used a large number of sources and combined them in a unique way.	Combining other people's words in a unique way is creative, but it is still plagiarism because the components of your construction are not your own. Imagine for a moment that you took a verse of a Beatles song, a chorus of a Stones song, and a bridge from a Who song and put them together in a "unique way" without citing the original contributions or gaining their prior approval to use their work.

1. My GPA and my accomplishments at the university show that I've learned enough to get my degree. I've met the intent of the assignment without doing the senior paper.

2. Whenever I try to present my position to faculty members, they always respond by saying, "rules are rules." Some rules are meant to be broken.

3. I've already been accepted to law school. Now the law school is threatening to rescind my acceptance. That's not fair.

4. I've had so many family problems this semester. My mother's very ill, and my dad's lost his job. I didn't have time to develop original critiques of all the pieces of literature in my paper.

3. Organizing Your Essay

Study this block diagram of a five-paragraph essay to plan a first draft of your essay. In your notebook, draw your own diagram and write your notes in each of its sections.

INTRODUCTION
Hook
General statements and/or summary of issue
Thesis statement

BODY ¶ 1
Argument
Apply ideas of appropriate philosopher as support

BODY ¶ 2
Counterargument
Apply ideas of appropriate philosopher as support

BODY ¶ 3
Refutation and new argument
Apply ideas of appropriate philosopher as support

CONCLUSION
Restate thesis
Summary of main points
Concluding thoughts

*Now write a **first draft** of your essay. Remember to write in complete sentences, and try to use some of the vocabulary and structures that you have practiced in this unit.*

C. Revising the First Draft

When you have finished writing the first draft, read it to a partner.

CHECKLIST FOR REVISING THE FIRST DRAFT

When you listen to your partner's essay and when you discuss your own, keep these questions in mind:

1. Does the thesis statement express the writer's point of view?

2. Does the writer clearly agree or disagree with at least one philosopher? Are arguments supported with information from the readings on the philosophers?

3. Does the writer include opposing arguments supported by the readings?

4. Does the writer refute the opposing arguments by explaining why they are wrong according to at least one of the philosophers?

5. Does the writer include at least one concession?

6. Does the conclusion summarize the writer's main arguments and leave the reader with something to think about?

After discussing your essay with a partner, you may want to reorganize your ideas or add more support based on the readings.

*Now write a **second draft** that includes all of your additions and changes.*

D. Editing the Second Draft

After you have written a second draft, proofread your work for any errors and correct them. These guidelines and exercises should help.

1. Unstated Conditionals

A teacher who catches one of her young students cheating might ask, "Mary, what would your parents say?" This question contains the main clause of a conditional but leaves out the if clause because it is understood.

"Mary, what would your parents say <u>if they knew you were cheating</u>?"

MAIN CLAUSE　　　　　　　　UNDERSTOOD *IF* CLAUSE

The *if* clause is also understood in the question, "What would Aristotle think about the issue of downloading?"

What would Aristotle think about downloading <u>if he were alive today</u>?

MAIN CLAUSE　　　　　　　　UNDERSTOOD *IF* CLAUSE

Answer these questions with complete if clauses.

1. How would Immanuel Kant feel about you reporting a friend whom you knew had cheated?

   Kant would *feel that it is essential for you to report cheating*

   if *you saw someone doing it.*

2. How would John Stuart Mill feel about someone breaking a pledge not to cheat?

   John Stuart Mill might _____

   _____

   if _____

   _____

3. How might someone in the recording industry react to thousands of students downloading music for free?

   A music producer might _____

   _____

   if _____

   _____

4. What if all students downloaded music and films without paying for them?

If all students _____

_____

_____ would/might _____

_____

5. What if everyone reported cheating?

_____

_____

if _____

_____

6. How would a filmmaker feel about people downloading a movie *after* they had paid to see it in a movie theater?

A filmmaker would probably feel _____

_____

_____

_____

7. What if you were a recording artist? How would you feel about people downloading your music without paying for it?

_____

_____

_____

_____

_____

2. Noun Clauses

A **noun clause** is a dependent clause that can be used as subject, object, or complement in a sentence. There are three types of noun clauses:

WH- NOUN CLAUSES

Wh- noun clauses are sometimes called **indirect questions or embedded questions**. They are formed from questions that begin with *who, what, where, how, when, why,* or *which*. Notice that these clauses use statement word order, so the auxiliary verbs that signal questions are no longer needed.

What **do students want**?
QUESTION

What **students want** more than anything is free stuff.
NOUN CLAUSE

Who **have you shared** files with?
QUESTION

Can they find out who **you've shared** files with?
NOUN CLA USE

IF / WHETHER NOUN CLAUSES

If / whether (or not) noun clauses are also sometimes called indirect questions or embedded questions. They are formed from *yes / no* questions and also use statement word order. These clauses can be introduced by *Whether (or not)* or *If . . . (or not)*.

I can't decide **whether or not** I should buy this song.
NOUN CLAUSE

Should I buy this song?   I can't decide **whether** I should buy this song **(or not)**.
QUESTION   NOUN CLAUSE

I can't decide **if** I should buy this song **(or not)**.
NOUN CLAUSE

As the subject of a sentence, use *Whether (or not)*.

Whether (or not) you buy it makes no difference to me.
NOUN CLAUSE

THAT CLAUSES

When a statement is used as a noun clause in another sentence, it is often introduced with the words *the fact that* or *that*.

Music companies make a lot of money. This shouldn't influence your decision.

The fact that music companies make a lot of money shouldn't influence your decision.
NOUN CLAUSE

In September 2003, the Recording Industry Association of America (RIAA) sued 261 individuals for as much as $150,000 per song for illegally swapping copies of songs over the Internet. The youngest person they sued was 12 years old, and the oldest was about 70 years old.

Write one or two new sentences by combining the ideas using noun clauses.

1. Why did they sue a 12-year-old girl? I can't understand that.

   I can't understand why the RIAA sued a 12-year-old girl.

   The fact that the RIAA sued a child is puzzling to many people.

2. They sued for up to $150,000 per song. That surprises me.

   _____

   _____

   _____

3. Should I continue to swap songs online? I can't decide.

   _____

   _____

   _____

4. Are universities legally responsible for what their students do? This is a question that troubles university officials.

   _____

   _____

   _____

5. No one close to me has gotten in trouble. This reassures me.

   _____

   _____

   _____

6. Four university students will have to pay between $12,000 and $17,500 to the recording industry. This disturbs me.

_____

_____

_____

7. Will those students be punished by university officials as well? Many students are wondering about this.

_____

_____

_____

8. Why do people continue to download without paying? It's not clear.

_____

_____

_____

9. Are music companies pursuing individual lawsuits abroad? This is something I'd like to know.

_____

_____

_____

10. How much online privacy do computer users have? We have a right to know.

_____

_____

_____

In your notebook, write ten sentences on any subject using different types of noun clauses. Share your sentences with a partner.

What bothers me about the lawsuits is that CDs are so expensive.

The fact that my roommate never washes his dishes drives me crazy.

E. Preparing the Final Draft

Reread your second draft and correct any errors you find. Put a check (✓) in each space as you edit for these points. Then write your corrected final version.

> ### CHECKLIST FOR EDITING THE SECOND DRAFT
>
> _____ unstated conditionals
>
> _____ noun clauses

V Additional Writing Opportunities

Write about one of the following topics.

1. Imagine you are a professor of media and communications at a reputable university. Write an essay in which you present the issue of downloading music and films off the Internet without paying for them from three different perspectives:

   - people in the recording and/or film industry

   - providers of Internet downloading services

   - people who use Internet downloading services

   Draw a conclusion about a policy for your university that you see as being the fairest to all concerned, and explain why you reached this conclusion.

2. In his writings, the philosopher Immanuel Kant said, "If you want to be moral, you must never contradict the personal rule that you use to make a decision." He insisted that there was no concept of "sometimes." Write an essay in which you examine the issue of lying, taking a stand on whether it is ever right to lie. Argue for or against Kant's position that being moral means being consistent in each and every instance.

3. Imagine that there is a scientist who has proven that he can make a drug that would cure all human disease. The vital ingredient of the drug, however, must be taken from a perfectly healthy child, and this child would die as a result. Write an essay in which you argue for or against the production of this drug. Cite the philosophers from this unit in your arguments.

4. What should an employee do if he knows that his boss is doing something illegal? Should he "blow the whistle" on his boss and risk losing his job, or should he keep it to himself and endanger the company or the public? Write an essay that discusses the moral aspects of each decision.

SUPPLEMENTARY ACTIVITIES

These suggestions come from our own classes and the classes of our colleagues.

UNIT 1
PANDORA'S BOX

Films for Listening and Discussion

1. Show students one of the movies listed below. You can choose to show portions of the films or divide the film into several 30- to 45-minute segments. Introduce each segment with vocabulary and some general discussion questions. Follow up the segments with comprehension questions. Prepared vocabulary lists and questions are often available on ESL websites.

- *Multiplicity* (1996), comedy. Michael Keaton plays one man and three of his clones.
- *Gattaca* (1997), sci-fi. A futuristic drama about a genetically imperfect man who has to fool the establishment in order to attain his goal of traveling into space.

Internet Research

2. Have students research topics related to current genetic engineering breakthroughs. Some topics that might be explored:

- stem-cell research, both in the United States and abroad
- cloning pets
- genetically engineered food
- the use of genetically altered animals for organ transplants

After researching a topic, students can take turns reporting to the class.

UNIT 2
CHERRIES FOR MY GRANDMA

Films for Listening and Discussion

1. Show students one of the movies listed below and use it as a basis of class discussion. You can also select just a portion of one film to use as a listening cloze. Scripts of certain films can often be found on the Internet, making it easy to create a cloze.

- *About a Boy* (2002), light drama. A young boy looks for a father substitute and finds an unlikely one in a wealthy but completely self-absorbed bachelor.
- *Music of the Heart* (1999), drama. A music student inspires her students.
- *The Joy Luck Club* (1993), drama. An examination of the influence mothers have on their daughters (use with excerpts from the book).

Listening to Songs

2. Go online and find the lyrics to the song "Because You Loved Me" (sung by Celine Dion) or "Hero" (sung by Mariah Carey). Then create a listening cloze for the students to fill in. Play the song several times so the students have ample time to complete the cloze. Have the students compare their answers with a partner while some students write the missing words on the board. Then correct the answers as a class. Finally play the song again. Singing along is optional.

Suggested Readings

3. Have students read different short stories from William Saroyan's *My Name is Aram*, such as "The Pomegranate Trees" or "The Summer of the Beautiful White Horse." After reading the stories, students should summarize the stories and present their summaries aloud in small groups. They should explain how the characters in their story influenced each other.

Internet Research

4. Have students research and report on a prominent figure who has inspired others, such as Nelson Mandela, Albert Schweitzer, Albert Einstein, Mother Teresa, or Mahatma Gandhi. After the reports, students can discuss which person they found the most inspiring and why they feel this way.

UNIT 3
THREE WORLDS IN ONE

Suggested Readings

1. Have students read three different theories on a historical event such as the Civil War and discuss which one seems most valid.

2. Have students read and discuss E.B. White's *Three New Yorks* and then devise three or four different categories for their own city. They can then discuss the scheme they have come up with the rest of the class.

Observation

3. Ask the students to take a trip to a local supermarket, park, or other pubic place and observe the people there for 20-30 minutes. Afterwards, they can categorize the people there according to the criteria they think best suits the data. They may, for example, decide there are three types of shoppers or four types of park goers.

Internet Research

4. Have the students go online to research the food and eating habits in three different parts of the world, then discuss them in small groups to see whether they can find a classification system different from that presented in the unit. Some suggestions:

- Papua New Guinea
- Santo Domingo, Dominican Republic
- Bangkok, Thailand
- Scotland, U.K
- Yucatan, Mexico

UNIT 4
WHO'S SPYING ON YOU?

Films for Listening and Discussion

1. There are many films which deal with the issue of privacy. You can choose to have students watch and discuss a classic film such as *1984* or *Brave New World*, or you can focus on more recent issues of privacy. Michael Crichton's book and movie *Indecent Proposal*, starring Michael Douglas and Demi Moore, takes an unusual look at sexual harassment at work. In the comedy, *Notting Hill*, Julia Roberts plays an actress whose life is being ruined by constant media attention. After watching the films, students can be assigned roles based on the characters in the films. These students can then be interviewed by the other students in the class.

Debating the Issues

2. Have students divide into two groups: those who are in favor of workplace monitoring and those who are opposed to it. Have members of each group list as many arguments as possible in support of their position. Use the readings to help prepare the arguments. Be sure each member has a different argument. Each group should also be prepared to refute the arguments of their opponents. Allow time for each student to present his argument, the opposing team to present a counterargument, and the first team to respond.

Internet Research

3. Have students research and report on current issues involving privacy. Some suggested topics:

- The use of satellite tracking devices in cars and cell phones
- The use of closed circuit television monitoring systems on public streets
- Computer programs that track consumer habits
- Security measures taken at airports and on public transportation
- New methods of identification being developed
- Identity theft prevention measures

UNIT 5
MIRROR, MIRROR, ON THE WALL

Films and TV Programs for Listening and Discussion

1. Have the students watch one or two episodes of a personal makeover program and discuss the changes that were made in the people's appearance, the way they felt about themselves before and after the changes, and the reasons for the show's popularity.

2. Show students one of the movies listed below or portions of it. You might choose to separate the films into segments so that the students can analyze the changes in the characters behavior and attitudes over the course of the movie. The follow-up discussion might focus on the relationship between appearance, personality, and behavior.

- *The Truth about Cats and Dogs*
- *Roxanne*
- *Never Been Kissed*

Trip to an Art Museum or Internet Research on Art from Different Periods

3. Have students visit an art museum and look at different artists' depictions of attractive women. The work of the following artists might illustrate how the concept of beauty changed over time and in different places: da Vinci, Rubens, Renoir, Gauguin, Modigliani, Botero. If there is no museum in the area, students may take a virtual trip to a museum on the Internet.

Internet Research

4. Have students research the case of Deborah Voight, the opera singer who was fired by Convent Garden in London for being overweight. Students might discuss whether the reasons given for dismissing Voight were valid.

UNIT 6
TWO THEORIES OF PERSONALITY TYPES

Reading and Discussion

1. Ask the students to take a personality quiz in a popular magazine or on the Internet. A follow-up discussion may focus on the types of questions in the quiz and the validity of the results.

Internet Research

2. Have the students research and report on different systems for determining an individual's personality, such as Numerology, Astrology and the Chinese Zodiac After the reports, students can discuss which. if any, of the systems seems the most valid.

Interviews

3. Ask students to interview people who work in Human Resources at a university, a hospital, a law firm, a bank, an advertising agency, a publishing company etc. about what types of people they feel are most successful in their respective fields and what types of questions they ask applicants to determine if they fit the profile. Students should discuss the results with the class and devise a list of qualifications the interviewees felt were desirable in each field.

UNIT 7
THE KITE RUNNER

Film Reviews

1. Have students choose a film to review. The film should include one of the themes from the excerpt of the Kite Runner. Students should view the film, and then write a review of the film that contains a short summary and the student's reaction to the film. Students might enjoy the following films:

- *Catch Me If You Can* (2002), starring Tom Hanks and Leonardo DiCaprio. DiCaprio is a con artist and son of a con artist who manages to elude the law through several career impersonations. Tom Hanks is the policeman assigned to catching him. The film examines the elusive father–son relationship.
- *Nobody's Fool* (1994), starring Paul Newman as the father. The film is set in a small town and describes how a father and son slowly reconcile as they work together. The film is based on a novel by Pulitzer prize winning novelist, Richard Russo.
- *Mad Hot Ballroom* (2005) is a delightful documentary about young students in the New York City public schools preparing for a city-wide dance competition. It follows the students through practices, and several rounds of the competition. Through interviews with several members of the dance groups, the audience is drawn into the lives of the children and the tension of the competition.

Role Play Interviews

2. Choose students to act as characters from *The Kite Runner*. Each student should prepare a short speech about his relationships with the other characters in the story. He can also discuss his role in the kite contest. The other students in the class should prepare questions for the various characters. Using a panel format, have the student actors present their short speeches and answer questions from the student audience.

UNIT 8
ETHICS IN THE DIGITAL AGE

Role Play

1. Have the students take on the roles of members of RIAA, movie theatre owners, owners of stores selling music and films, singers, songwriters, owners of radio stations, university administrators, and professors. Ask them to discuss the issue of illegal downloading and come up with a policy that all (or most) of them can live with.

Internet Research

2. Have students research recent developments with respect to the issue of downloading and file sharing. Ask them to create a timeline spanning the last five years and make some predictions about what the future holds with respect to this issue.

Reading and Discussion

3. Have the students read selections from Randy Cohen's "The Good, The Bad and the Difference," summarize two or three of the reader's dilemmas, and decide what choice is the most ethical in each case.

Have the students read two or three other cases devised by social psychologist Lawrence Kohlberg and decide which choice they would consider to be the most moral in each situation.

Films for Discussion

4. Have the students summarize the moral dilemma in these films and come to a conclusion about what, in each case, is the most ethical course.

- *Dinner with Friends* (Donald Margulies, 2001; can be used with the play script)
- *Crimes and Misdemeanors* (Woody Allen, 1989)
- *An Enemy of the People* (play by Henrik Ibsen, adapted by Arthur Miller, 1966, and by Alexander Jacobs, 1978; can be used with the play script)

ANSWER KEY

UNIT 1
PANDORA'S BOX

II. Reading for Writing
A. General Understanding (p. 5)
1. Identifying Arguments
(Answers will vary.)

Benefits of cloning
1. A clone could provide a perfect match for a bone marrow transplant.
2. Parents could guarantee that they wouldn't pass on a serious genetic condition to their child.
3. Sterile parents can have a biological child.

Fears about cloning
1. Parents will choose only the traits that they want in a child.
2. Cloning experiments with humans could produce malformed babies.
3. No one knows what issues will arise from raising a generation of cloned children.

2. Making Inferences
(Answers will vary.)
1. Human cloning is now more possible. Because of this, the moral and ethical questions have to be discussed.
2. People will try to create a perfect child and eventually all children will be very similar to each other.
3. Using dead cells to clone a person from history will not produce the same type of person in the present.
4. The author uses words such as "frightening," "repugnant," "unthinkable" when talking about cloning. Also, he raises questions about the value of cloning extinct species and the cultural problems of a cloned generation.

B. Working with Language (p. 6)
1. Word Search
a. sterile
b. ethical
c. narcissistic
d. justify
e. cut and dried
f. immoral
g. implications
h. extinct
i. species
j. identity

2. Word Forms
a. ethics; ethical; ethically
b. extinction
c. immorality; immorally
d. justification; justified
e. narcissist, narcissism
f. sterility; sterilize
g. cloning; clone; cloned

3. Reproductive and Therapeutic Cloning
1. cloning
2. repugnant
3. narcissism
4. ethically
5. justifies
6. immoral
7. cut and dried
8. implications
9. extinction
10. species

III. Prewriting Activities
A. Collecting Support for Arguments (p. 8)
For cloning: 2, 7, 8
Against cloning: 1, 5, 6
Neither/Both: 3, 4

IV. Structured Writing Focus
B. Preparing the First Draft (p. 11)
2. Analyzing a Summary Paragraph
1. Topic sentence: "In this cartoon from The New York Times newspaper, the artist is trying to show in a comical way the advantages and disadvantages of cloning." It says what the cartoon is about.
2. The concluding sentence repeats the same idea as the first sentence.
Concluding sentence: "In this cartoon, the artist shows us both positive and negative possibilities for cloning."
3. The other sentences—the body of the paragraph—contain the information that supports the main topic.
Body: all sentences between the first and last sentence.

4. Analyzing a Response Paragraph
   1. The first sentence. He believes that cloning can be harmful to society.
   2. He says that "when scientists interfere with nature they usually create new problems," and "If employees always think exactly like their boss, there will be fewer new ideas in a company." His support is based on the cartoon.
   3. harmful

D. Editing the Second Draft (p. 16)
1. Expressing Another Person's Opinion
   (Answers will vary.)
   2. Summary: Robert Oppenhiemer, one of the creators of the atomic bomb, says that you should always take the opportunity to develop new technologies.
   Response: This is true because it is human nature to attempt what is possible. There has never been a case where people could do or make something but didn't.
   3. Summary: Former president of the United States Bill Clinton thinks that humans should not be cloned because human life cannot be created in a laboratory.
   Response: This view is idealistic and perhaps even morally correct, but it is also unlikely to be followed. Replicating ourselves will surely prove to great a temptation to resist.
   4. Summary: Nobel Prize winner and genetic scientist Dr. James Watson states that the decisions about cloning should not be made by doctors and scientists alone.
   Response: For a scientist to recognize and warn against the dangers of leaving the decisions about cloning in the hands of scientists says a lot. If a scientist does not trust his peers to use cloning technology responsibly, then surely the public also must question what is happening in laboratories and research institutions.

2. Subject-Verb Agreement
   2. This amendment **protects** the right of freedom of speech.
   3. A legal scholar from the University of Chicago **argues** that . . .
   4. He **maintains** that the founding fathers were concerned . . .
   5. . . . and the members of the Supreme Court today also **have** a high regard for it.

   6. Arguments in favor of defending . . . **are** complex.
   7–10. One of the many legal scholars involved **says** that raising questions that **challenge** and **explore** cultural norms is exactly the kind of research the founding fathers wanted to encourage.
   11. . . . only if the studies in question **threaten** national security . . .
   12–13. While releasing smallpox into the air to see how it spreads **is** clearly a threat and should be banned, conducting stem cell experiments **does not** present a clear danger to public health or security.

UNIT 2
CHERRIES FOR MY GRANDMA

II. Reading for Writing
A. General Understanding (p. 24)
1. Understanding the Reading
   1. a, d
   2. a. 2, 3, 10, 13
      b. 6, 7, 14
      c. 3, 4
      d. 1, 5, 13
   3. *(Answers will vary.)*

B. Working with Language (p. 26)
1. Identifying Synonyms
   2. injure, harm
   3. honor
   4. firm
   5. careless, irresponsible
   6. dream, imagine
   7. strong, difficult
   8. pity, love, concern
   9. greedy
   10. avoid, delay, postpone

2. Word Forms
   1. sacrifice; sacrificing; sacrificial
   2. dignify; dignified
   3. target; targeted
   4. determination; determine
   5. recklessness; recklessly
   6. compassion; compassionately
   7. materialism; materialistically
   8. fantasy; fantastic
   9. toughness; toughen; tough
   10. strain; strained

3. Describing Characters

(*Answers will vary.*)

Geoffrey Canada: kind, intelligent, talented

His mother: hard-working, moral, compassionate, poor, tough, determined, sacrificing

His grandmother: hard-working, moral, compassionate, poor, tough, determined, sacrificing, dignified, beautiful, intelligent

His grandfather: moral, hard-working

4. Writing a Summary

(*Answers will vary.*)

In "Cherries for My Grandma," Geoffrey Canada talks about the sacrifices his mother and grandmother made when he was growing up, even though he and his brothers didn't always realize or appreciate these sacrifices until much later. He also discusses the many lessons he learned from these women and the powerful influence they have had on his life. Canada now knows how hard-working, determined, and compassionate his mother and grandmother were, and how he has benefited from these qualities in them.

III. Prewriting Activities

A. Recognizing Detailed Descriptions (p. 28)

1. a. 17–20
   b. 6–9
   h. 2–4, 8–9
   j. 5, 11–13, 18–20
   k. 7–9
   m. 15, 22
   p. 22–23

IV. Structured Writing Focus

B. Preparing the First Draft (p. 31)

1. Analyzing Essay Structure

(*Answers will vary.*)

First Draft

1. The hook is not very interesting. She should add details.

2. Thesis statement: "I never realized until I became a grown-up myself how much influence she had on me." She should give the reader an idea of what to expect in the body paragraphs. This sounds as if she will only discuss her aunt's influence on her adult life.

3. Paragraphs 2–4 start with a topic sentence related to the writer's age. Paragraph

4 discusses her aunt's influence on her adult life and also acts as a conclusion.

4. She wanted to look like her aunt. Her aunt taught her about fashion.

5. her aunt's job; the aunt's personality

6. seeing: her aunt's snow-white skin and elegant look, drawing a perfect eye line; hearing: conversation, telling her this and that; the writer could appeal to more senses and give more details of her experiences with her aunt

7. The paragraphs follow logically because they are chronological. However, there is a transition missing from her adolescent resentment to her adult gratitude.

8. The conclusion restates her affection for her aunt, but it does not summarize how her aunt influenced her. She does not unify the essay with words or phrases from the introduction.

9. The paragraphs are not indented. There are four paragraphs rather than five. The last paragraph is part body paragraph and part conclusion.

Second Draft

1. She has made the hook more interesting by adding details and by setting up a comparison.

2. Yes; the thesis statement tells us the structure of the body paragraphs (childhood, teenage years, adult life/career) and the influence her aunt had at each step.

3. She gives more detailed descriptions and appeals to more senses.

4. The fourth paragraph discusses the latest way that her aunt has influenced her. It allows the fifth paragraph to be the conclusion.

5. The second title is better. It helps to unify the essay because this phrase is repeated in the last sentence.

6. Yes. She says that her aunt influenced her throughout her life.

7. This is a standard five-paragraph essay. The paragraphs are clearly indented to separate ideas.

2. Practice with Hooks

(*Answers will vary.*)

3. This is a good hook because it is strong and catches the reader's attention. We are curious about who said this and why.

4. This is not a very interesting hook. It doesn't include anything to make us interested in this person or his/her influence.

5. This is a good hook. It asks a question that immediately involves the reader in the answer. Either the reader can relate to the question or wants to find out more.

6. This is not a very good hook. It is too general.

7. This is a good hook because it is mysterious. The reader wonders who "he" is, how he died, and why his death was important to the writer.

3. Practice with Thesis Statements
(Answers will vary.)

2. This is not such a good thesis statement because the reader has no idea what the essay will be about.

3. This is a good thesis statement because we can anticipate the structure of the essay. The writer will talk about how each type of flower symbolized a different type of love or a different way that "he" showed his love. We are curious about the symbolism the writer will use.

4. This is not a good thesis statement. It does not lead us to the next paragraphs but only seems to finish a thought from the introduction.

5. This thesis statement tells the reader about the structure but it is not interesting. It does not make us curious about what is to come.

6. This is a good thesis statement. It tells us how the essay will be structured and who the essay is about. It also tells us something personal about the writer, which makes us want to learn more.

7. This is a good thesis statement because it makes us curious to read about what happened.

8. This is a good thesis statement because it sets up the whole essay. We know what will be discussed in each of the body paragraphs, and we know the writer will relate these points to all people.

4. Using a Summary as an Introduction
(Answers will vary.)

1. The title and author of the work that the writer is summarizing. It also tells us the topic. The writer uses clues to arouse our interest.

2. the dignity of hard work, the love of beauty, and the importance of family

3. The writer relates the themes of the Soto essay to his own life. The last sentence moves the reader away from Soto's story and into the writer's own life.

5. Supporting Your Opinions with Detailed Examples

2. His mother never went to the movies. She made her own clothes. She went without lunch. She didn't go to college until later in life. She walked instead of taking the bus.

3. He says there was much love in his family.

4. She taught him to have a deep spiritual love of life. He says she saved his soul.

5. He would fantasize about buying her all the cherries she could eat.

6. He says that he was wild and reckless.

D. Editing the Second Draft (p. 40)

1. Adjective Clauses: Restrictive and Nonrestrictive
(Answers will vary.)
Soto sets off information in commas when it is not directly related to the sentence.

2. Habitual Past: *used to* vs. *would*

1. a, b; both of these could be used as a comparison of the past and now, or they could be details about a past time.

2. c; this is only describing a situation that was true in the past but is not true now.

(Answers will vary.)

When I think about my childhood, the person who comes right into my head is my Aunt Eloise. My sisters and I **used to call** her Eloista. She was more than our nanny. My parents were hard-working people. They didn't have time to take care of us, so my aunt **used to come** to our house every morning. She **would bring** newly baked bread for breakfast. She **would help** us to get ready to go to school. She **would prepare** my lunchbox and sometimes even **braid** my hair. We **would come** back from school to her delicious food. Nobody could cook like she did. She was famous for her tasty roast beef and an Italian soup called "minestrone". We **used to have** a kitten in our yard, and Aunt Eloista **would feed** her leftover bits of the wonderful meals she cooked.

II. Reading for Writing
A. General Understanding (p. 48)
1. Understanding the Main Ideas
1. False. Fork-feeders are outnumbered 2 to 1.
2. True
3. False. Some rulers continued to eat with their fingers: Queen Elizabeth I of England, Louis XIV of France.
4. True
5. False. Areas and social classes with the highest birthrates in the world shun forks.

2. Categorizing Information
Fingers

Regions in which it is used: Africa, the Middle East, Indonesia, and the Indian subcontinent

Reason for the preference: (not specifically stated in reading; answers will vary)

Any change in preference over time, and why: sometimes the fork is a status marker

Forks

Regions in which it is used: Europe and North America

Reason for the preference: made it easier to handle hot food; status marker

Any change in preference over time, and why: resurgence of ethnic pride

Chopsticks

Regions in which it is used: Eastern Asia

Reason for the preference: portions were small and did not have to be cut

Any change in preference over time, and why: sometimes use fork around Western guests

3. Summarizing Information
(Answers will vary.)

The world is divided into three eating methods: fork, fingers, and chopsticks. The reasons for these different methods have to do with the type and temperature of food, and the social status of the eater. However, preferences for each method have changed over time in different parts of the world.

B. Working with Language (p. 49)
1. Avoiding Repetition with Synonyms
1. a. ways of putting solid food into the mouth
   b. utensil, implement
   c. instrument
2. cuisine
3. resurgence
4. crowned head, potentates

2. Reviewing Vocabulary
2. resurgence
3. pride
4. globalization
5. chauvinism
6. shunned
7. status marker

III. Prewriting Activities
A. Chronological Classification (p. 51)
1. Understanding the Classification
2. 3rd wave; people's lives are not so regular as in the past because they can work anywhere and anytime
3. 1st wave; life is based on agriculture and the gathering of food. The seasons rule their lives.
4. 3rd wave; this period of time is marked by a "brain force" economy, so education is more important to common people than in the past
5. 2nd wave; many people moved from farm areas to cities and worked in factories
6. 1st wave; people were generalists and learned all the skills they needed for their lives from each other

IV. Structured Writing Focus
B. Preparing the First Draft (p. 55)
1. Deciding on a Principle of Organization
2. . . . how they get money to operate the station (advertising, contributions and grants, subscribers)
3. . . . the involvement of the rider (self-propelled, operator, passenger)
4. . . . how many people are required in order to play
5. . . . what they eat (plants, meat/other animals, both)
6. . . . geographical characteristics
7. . . . who or what is worshipped and how

2. Identifying Overlap
2. Curly hair and straight hair can both be fashionable.
3. Comedies and dramas can both be independently made.

4. Large and mid-size cities can both be coastal.

5. Boys' and girls' toys can both be educational.

6. Farming and manufacturing are both types of businesses.

3. Analyzing a Classification Essay

(Some answers will vary.)

1. Yes. Three types of people in the world.

2. People's behavior with umbrellas.

3. There are some people who only take an umbrella sometimes. He says they are few and difficult to identify.

4. It will help us better understand human nature as a whole.

5. It is satirizing making judgments using superficial characteristics of someone or something. There is no real connection.

Body paragraph 1

1. They are inflexible, have a lot of anxiety and need to control things.

2. They feel they have control over the weather.

3. The last sentence. It talks about the next group.

Body paragraph 2

1. They are carefree and optimistic, they are not controlling, and they don't think ahead.

2. They don't try to control their environment.

3. The writer extends NTUs' carefree attitude to toward the weather to family planning, which is much more serious.

4. The last sentence. It talks about the next group.

Body paragraph 3

1. They have a practical, instrumental attitude to life.

2. For them, umbrellas carry no symbolic importance.

3. Because they can sometimes be mistaken for NTUs or ATUs, and are the hardest to distinguish.

4. The writer characterizes STUs as "elusive" but they are really like most people.

Conclusion

(Answers will vary.)

D. Editing the Second Draft (p. 63)

2. those

3. one

4. that

5. This / It

6. This / That

Europe in the Middle Ages

2. one

3. It / This

4. It / This

5. It / This

6. They / These

7. this / it

8. These

9. These / They

10. These / They

11. ones

UNIT 4
WHO'S SPYING ON YOU?

II. Reading for Writing
A. General Understanding (p. 70)
1. Understanding the Reading

(Answers will vary.)

1. It's about how some companies are tracking employees' e-mail usage.

2. Mr. Quinn: He thinks it's a good way to find out why the system keeps crashing.

Mr. Gruber: He thinks it's dangerous for the company to have this information.

Ms. Trainor: She thinks it's an invasion of privacy, but that there is a good reason to do it.

3. It recommends that employers let employees know their e-mail is being monitored.

2. Why Do Companies Monitor Office E-mail?

2. e   3. d   4. f   5. c   6. a

B. Working with Language (p. 72)
1. Vocabulary in Context

Jerry: 2. b 3. a

Jane: 1. b 2. d 3. c 4. e 5. a

Anna: 1. b 2. a 3. e 4. d 5. c

III. Prewriting Activities
A. Summarizing and Responding to Academic Research (p. 74)

Excerpt 1:

1. they have almost none
2. The technology exists to make this kind of society, and workplace, possible.

Excerpt 2:

1. passivity, feelings of powerlessness, loneliness, and free-floating anxiety
2. with conformity
3. depression and nervous breakdown

Excerpt 3:

1. low motivation, poor performance, difficulty with goal-setting, and poor reactions to supervisory feedback
2. constantly scan worker attitudes towards reduced privacy; possible results of good and bad workplace privacy practices

IV. Structured Writing Focus

B. Preparing the First Draft (p. 80)

1. Using a Summary as the Introduction to an Essay

1. "and the clocks were striking thirteen." It's interesting because clocks in our society don't strike thirteen.
2. The topic of the essay.
3. The last sentence is the thesis statement. It's direct.

2. Using the Conclusion to Unify Your Essay

1. "Technology has changed for the better the way we work today"; technology, better, today; changed it into a question
2. He says that with monitoring the workplace would be less efficient and more dangerous. He asks how the reader would feel if they owned a company.
3. employers can prevent wasted time; workplaces are more efficient, less dangerous
4. It invites the reader to think about all the writer's points.

D. Editing the Second Draft (p. 84)

1. article titles from newspapers, magazines, and scholarly journals
2. books, newspapers, magazines, and scholarly journals
3. Last name, comma, first name

Works Cited

Bandura, A. Social Learning Theory. Englewood Cliffs, NJ: Prentice Hall, 1977.

Brown, William S. "Technology, Workplace Privacy and Personhood." Journal of Business Ethics 15 (1996): 1237-39, 1250-53.

Foucault, M. Discipline and Punish: The Birth of Prison. New York: Vintage Books, 1979.

Fromm, Erich. Escape from Freedom. New York: Avon Books, 1968.

Howard, R. Brave New Workplace. New York: Viking Books, 1985.

Kilborn, P. T. "Abuse of Sick Leave Rises and Companies Fight Back," The New York Times 30 Nov. 1992, final edition: A12.

Simon, H. A. "What Computers Mean for Man and Society." Science March 18 (1977): 86-91.

Zuboff, S. In the Age of the Smart Machine: The Future of Work and Power. New York: Basic Books, 1988.

UNIT 5
MIRROR, MIRROR, ON THE WALL

II. Reading for Writing

A. General Understanding (p. 92)

1. Understanding the Main Idea

Answers will vary. One example is:
Beautiful people have an easier life than less attractive people.

2. Identifying Support

1. True
2. False
3. True
4. True
5. False
6. False
7. False
8. True

3. Writing Up Research Studies

(Answers will vary on some items.)

Prison Study

Results: participants who received cosmetic surgery were less likely to return to prison.

Explanation: more attractive people are treated better in society, so they are less likely to have reason to commit crimes and are less likely to be convicted for crimes.

Business Study

Participants: job applicants

Aim of study: to see whether attractive people are hired more often than less attractive people

Procedure: different photos were attached to identical job applications

Results: the more attractive people were more likely to be hired

Explanation: employers assume that attractive people are more capable and intelligent so attractive people have more and better job opportunities

Education Study

Participants: teachers

Aim of study: to see whether teachers discriminate against children based on attractiveness

Procedure: different photos were attached to identical student records

Results: teachers more often judged the less attractive child to be a slow learner

Explanation: attractive children are favored by teachers and get more attention and positive reinforcement in school

B. Working with Language (p. 94)

1. Understanding Euphemisms

Fat: big-boned, full-figured, husky, plump, stout

Old: of a certain age, senior, veteran

Ugly: dowdy, homely, not terribly attractive, plain, unremarkable

Short: compact, diminutive, slight of build

4. Building Cause-and-Effect Sentences

(Answers will vary.)

2. . . . leads to unattractive people being discriminated against.

3. . . . consequently, they are at a disadvantage when competing for jobs against attractive people.

4. . . . that they sometimes come to believe they deserve it.

5. Because/Since . . . attractive children do better in school.

III. Prewriting Activities

A. Identifying Cause and Effect (p. 98)

(Sentences will vary.)

2. a. effect   b. cause

Because people feel self-conscious about the way they look, they often decide to undergo cosmetic surgery.

3. a. cause   b. effect

Psychologist Thomas F. Cash found that young children quickly absorb definitions of attractiveness; as a result, when children do not conform to these standards, they may be teased.

4. a. cause   b. effect

As they grow up, children develop a great loss of self-esteem; as a result, as grown-ups, they develop deep depression.

5. a. cause   b. effect

People develop eating disorders because they were teased a lot as children about their weight.

6. a. effect   b. cause

Children are teased or criticized by parents, older siblings, teachers, coaches or other significant people in their lives; consequently, they become intensely self-conscious about their defect

7. a. effect   b. cause

People want to get help identifying and changing unrealistic thinking patterns. Because of this, they are turning to psychological therapy.

B. Preparing the First Draft (p. 101)

(Answers will vary.)

1. "SAFER"

Statistics: in a study of 17,000 men, those who are at least six-foot-tall did better professionally than shorter men

Anecdotes: in fairy tales, good people are usually pretty and bad people are usually ugly; Cleopatra and Helen of Troy

Facts: attractive people do better in school, at work, and in society; men who are with pretty women are considered more intelligent and successful by strangers; taller men are more successful professionally and personally than shorter men

Examples: handsome West Point cadets graduated with a higher rank; the prison study; the business study; the education study; the unattractive man / pretty woman study; the beauty of Cleopatra and Helen of Troy influenced politics

Reasons: fairy tales instill the idea that beauty reflects goodness; attractive children receive more attention and praise from adults; tall men trigger a childhood response to authority figures

D. Editing the Second Draft (p. 107)

1. Causal Connectors

(Answers will vary.)

2. teasing → negative body image

When children tease another child about his or her appearance, that child can develop a negative body image.

3. low self-esteem → negative body image
   Many people who have a negative body image because of low self-esteem.
   low self-esteem   negative body image
   A person with low self-esteem can generalize his or her bad feelings to their appearance, resulting in a negative body image.

4. eating disorders   low self-esteem
   Low self-esteem can lead to many health problems, such as eating disorders.

5. emphasis on thinness in the media → self-consciousness
   Self-consciousness about physical "imperfections" is often the result of the emphasis on thinness in movies, television, and advertising.

6. cosmetic surgery   self-consciousness
   Some people who are self-conscious about a physical imperfection choose to get plastic surgery to correct it.

7. increase in self-esteem   cosmetic surgery
   Cosmetic surgery can make a person feel better about his or her appearance, resulting in an increase in self-esteem.

UNIT 6
TWO THEORIES OF PERSONALITY TYPES

II. Reading for Writing
A. General Understanding, Part A (p. 114)
1. Categorizing Somatotypes and Personality Traits
   1. Endomorphic: soft, round body; good-humored, relaxed, tolerant
   Mesomorphic: hard, muscular body; active, combative, courageous,
   Ectomorphic: thin, delicate body; introverted, quiet, sensitive

B. Working with Language (p. 117)
1. Understanding Prefixes and Suffixes
   1. c   2. e   3. b   4. a   5. d
2. Building Words with Prefixes and Suffixes
   1. introverted: quiet and shy; *intro-*: into, inward; *-vert*: turn, direct
   2. extroverted: cheerful, social; *extro-*: outward
   3. circulate: to go from one person or group to another, to move around; *circu-*: circle, ring

4. psychosomatic: imaginary, formed in the mind; *psych-* or *psycho-*: mental, about or from the mind
5. metamorphosis: a complete change of form; *meta-*: change, transformation

A. General Understanding, Part B (p. 121)
1. Categorizing Personality Traits
   2. TF   3. JP   4. NS

III. Prewriting Activities
A. Sheldon's Theory (p. 123)
1. Summarizing Sheldon's Theory
   2. 3 main types, with 7 primary subtypes and infinitive variations
   3. mesomorphic: hard and muscular; ectomorphic: thin and delicate; endomorphic: soft and and round
   4. subjective assessment: observation and in-depth interviews
   5. 3 main types
   6. endotonia: love of relaxation, comfort, food, and people; mesotonia: centered on assertiveness and a love of action; ectotonia: focused on privacy, restraint, and highly developed self-awareness
   7. 7 primary subtypes and infinite variations

B. The Myers-Briggs Theory (p. 124)
1. Summarizing the Myers-Briggs Theory
   2. self-assessment questionnaires
   3. 8 (four sets of 2 traits)
   4. Extroversion–Introversion, Intuition–Sensing, Thinking–Feeling, Judgment–Perception
   5. 16
   6. subjectively, by determining the combination of traits

IV. Structured Writing Focus
A. Starting to Write (p. 125)
1. Brainstorming
   (*Some answers will vary.*)
   2. yes; yes   3. yes; yes   4. no; no
   5. no; yes   6. yes; no   10. no; yes
2. Comparing and Contrasting Theories
   (*Some answers will vary.*)
   1. theory; theory
   2. 3 main, 7 sub, variations; 16

B. Preparing the First Draft (p. 127)
1. Introductory Paragraphs for Comparison and Contrast Essays
   1. yes; the first line (the question)

2. Both theories are flawed.

3. The writer does not think they are credible.

4. Similar, neither, both, common/on the other hand, different

5. It mentions a "common" assertion but "different" typologies

D. Editing the Second Draft (p. 130)

1. Clauses of Comparison, Contrast, and Concession

(Answers will vary)

1. Numerologists often use the number of letters in a person's name to create a personality profile, while astrologers use people's birth date to create personality profiles for them.

2. Many people enjoy taking personality tests in magazines, even though few people have much faith in them.

3. Sheldon's endomorphs are lively, social people who enjoy parties, similar to Myers-Briggs' extroverts, who enjoy human contact and social situations.

4. Although serious astrologers base their analyses on careful study, they are not scientists and have no expertise in drawing larger conclusions from their observations.

5. Handwriting analysis claims to examine personality based on a physical manifestation of subconscious temperament, in contrast to Sheldon, who claimed to analyze personality based on the physical manifestation of subconscious temperament.

2. Transitional Expressions Between Sentences

(Answers will vary.)

1. Numerologists use numbers to chart a person's personality; in contrast, astrologers use birthdates to chart personalities.

2. The western zodiac describes people's personalities in terms of animals, occupations, and objects; the Chinese zodiac, on the other hand, describes people's personalities only in terms of animals.

3. In Asia, the meaning of the Chinese characters in a person's name reflects the parents' hopes for the child's future; in the same way, in Western countries, children's names are often chosen to reflect their parents' hopes for their future.

4. The MBTI depends on people's honesty and their ability to accurately assess their own attitudes and behaviors; conversely, astrology depends on fixed and confirmable data about a person's birth and the positions of different celestial bodies.

5. Handwriting analysis strives to tell people something about their own characters; in the same way, astrology hopes to give people insight into their own potential and limits.

UNIT 7
THE KITE RUNNER

III. Prewriting Activities

B. Understanding the Story (p. 144)

1. Building Tension

Correct order: 1, 5, 6, 4, 2, 3

2. Analyzing Descriptive Language

(Answers will vary.)

Hearing: the crowd cheering, the kite runners yelling, music, the blood in his head, the kite flapping like a bird, Amir screaming

Seeing: the color of the kites, the kites flying and falling, the clear blue sky

Smelling: the smell of food from rooftops and doorways, sharks roaming for prey, the smell of victory

Tasting: people on the rooftops sipping tea from thermoses

Touching: the glass strings cutting his hands, the spool rolling in his hands, the temperature getting colder, embracing

3. Making Inferences

(Answers will vary.)

1. a. He felt unimportant before but now this could change.

b. He had felt helpless for so long, but now he felt hope.

c. He knew that he was going to win for sure.

d. His victory would wipe away past feelings of failure.

2. They have great affection for each other. Their friendship ends somehow because Amir says that he would not see his friend smile for another 26 years. Also, the last three lines imply in an ironic way that

things would not be happy in the future.

3. He thinks his father will finally be proud of him. He wishes they could live "happily ever after," but his last line implies that they will not.

C. Working with Language (p. 147)

1. Using New Words

1. dwindled
2. glared
3. pack it in
4. putting myself through this
5. huddled
6. stole a glance
7. didn't dare
8. an open book
9. gaze

IV. Structured Writing Focus

A. Starting to Write

1. Brainstorming

For the alternative task (p. 150)

1. a, b, e   2. a, b, e   3. a, b, d

B. Preparing the First Draft (p. 152)

1. Introducing a Literary Analysis Essay

(Answers will vary.)

1. a quote
2. Yes. He talks about fathers and sons in general, then relates those comments to *The Kite Runner.*
3. He added the title of the book. This clearly relates his comments to the characters in the book.
4. He adds a brief summary of the story to prepare the reader for the relationships he is going to discuss in the essay.

2. Using Quotes from the Text as Support

(Answers will vary.)

1. 4; The quotes give concrete examples from the text to support his points.
2. The first two quotes are sandwiched between one introduction and one explanation (the presence and absence of Amir's father and Amir's struggle to get positive feedback from him). The third quote also has an introduction and an explanation. The last quote is used to illustrate the point the writer wants to make about all people.
3. The ending punctuation goes after the line number citation for a statement. A question mark goes inside the ending

quotation mark and a period follows the line number.

3. Understanding Figurative Language

(Other answers may also be possible.)

Simile: lines 20, 32, 65–6, 104–5, 109, 115–7, 130, 183, 229

Metaphor: lines 74–5, 79, 94, 108, 131–2, 192, 204–5, 231–2, 266–8

Personification: lines 40–1, 129, 145, 149, 161, 163–4, 181–2

D. Editing the Second Draft (p. 159)

(Answers will vary.)

1. **might have felt** differently about Hassan. **might not have felt** as close to Amir.
2. **wouldn't have followed** Amir into the water because he couldn't swim.

1. past unreal conditional: If Amir **had slept** well the night before the kite-running contest, he **wouldn't have been** mean to Hassan.
2. present unreal conditional: If Hassan **didn't understand** Amir better than Amir understands himself, Amir **would** need to apologize to Hassan for being mean.
3. past unreal conditional: If Amir **hadn't wanted** very much to gain his father's approval, he **wouldn't have been** extremely nervous before the kite contest.
4. present unreal conditional: If Hassan didn't tell Amir his dream about the monster in the lake, Amir wouldn't have the courage to enter the contest.
5. present unreal conditional: If Amir **were closer** to his father, he **wouldn't wonder** whether his father **wants** him to fail in the kite contest.

UNIT 8
ETHICS IN THE DIGITAL AGE

II. Reading for Writing

A. General Understanding (p. 166)

1. What do you think?

(Some answers will vary.)

1. The university's policy is not to allow illegal downloading. It sends messages to students to remind them of the policy. Also, students must take an online tutorial and indicate that they have read and agree to the policy.
2. Students have largely ignored the

university's policy on downloading. Because Internet access is easily accessible and so many student materials are available online, they see this as an invitation to use the university system to download from the Internet as well.

B. Working with Language (p. 168)

1. Using Context Clues

1. d   2. f   3. e   4. c   5. a   6. b

1. excessive
2. pragmatic
3. copyright
4. grasping
5. monitor
6. urge

2. Idioms in Context

1. to draw the line
2. has taken a harder line
3. going online
4. blurring the lines between right and wrong

III. Prewriting Activities

A. Theories of Ethics (p. 170)

1. Synthesizing Information

(Answers will vary.)

Immanuel Kant

1. He would be against it. You should never lie for any reason.
2. Kant would also consider this a lie, so he would be against it.

John Stuart Mill

1. You should save the person if doing so would prevent that person's suffering and not cause you or anyone else suffering.
2. If the patients would feel good about possibly helping others, and the drug really does have great potential to relieve the suffering of others, Mill would say it's OK. He would probably be in favor of forcing the patients to be test subjects against their will as well, if the resulting drug would greatly benefit many more people.

Aristotle

1. He would say the person's growth might be stunted because social relationships are necessary for human development.
2. He might have asked that person what kind of person they wanted to be. If being a thief, no matter the reason, was not what

they wanted to be, they shouldn't steal.

2. Comparing Kant, Mill, and Aristotle

(Answers will vary.)

Kant: No. Stealing is a form of lying, and lying for any reason is wrong.

Mill: No. The artists suffer because they are not being paid for their work.

Yes: Music brings happiness to the many people who listen to it. More people benefit from listening to the music than industry people and artists benefit from selling it.

Aristotle: No. Downloading is against the laws of the society in which we live. This interferes with a person's social development.

Yes. For people who feel no guilt for taking something they perceive to be free, downloading would not be an unethical act. If they do not perceive themselves to be thieves, then it doesn't interfere with their social development. They might even use the music they download to enhance social relationships by sharing files and enjoying the music in social situations.

IV. Structured Writing Focus

B. Preparing the First Draft (p. 176)

1. Analyzing an Argumentative Essay

I. Introduction

A. Is it wrong to hand in someone else's work as your own?

B. 2. we often ignore the morality of a situation; 3. we often do things that are best for us in the moment

C. With the support of Kant and Aristotle, the case against John's actions is made even stronger.

II. Body Paragraphs

A. Argument 1

1. a. lying is a form of manipulation; c. it is wrong to lie under any circumstances; d. what if everyone acted this way?
2. b. John violated the trust of his professor and made a fool of him as well

B. Counterargument

b. John was able to complete the course and graduate on time; c. John's future students were helped by having a good English teacher

Refutation: It is dangerous to accept

a philosophy that encourages people to believe that the end justifies the means.

C. Refutation/Argument 2

Support 1. b. he never learned whether he could have answered that question on his own; c. he never had the satisfaction of receiving a grade based on his own work; d. he will always look back on this incident with shame and regret

Support 2. a. John hurt himself, which is obvious by his regret; b. his action made it harder for him to mature into a person he could respect

III. Conclusion

A. Our instincts tell us John was wrong to submit Carol's work as his own, and our instincts are right.

B. wrong, lie

C. 1. it was wrong for John to focus only on the consequences of failing to complete the assignment; 3. even though it is easy to argue that the end justifies the means, it can also put us in the position of being untrue to ourselves

D. 1. John should have thought about the person he wanted to become

D. Editing the Second Draft (p. 184)

1. Unstated Conditionals

(Answers will vary.)

2. feel it was justified / most of the people involved in the situation benefited.

3. try to have downloaders arrested / he was losing a lot of money.

4. downloaded music and movies without paying, the music and movie companies / develop technologies to make downloading more difficult.

5. cheating would probably stop / everyone reported it.

6. that this was still stealing because the person would not pay to see the movie again nor rent the DVD later.

2. Noun clauses

(Answers will vary.)

2. It surprises me that they sued for up to $150,000 per song.

3. I can't decide if I should continue to swap songs online.

4. A question that troubles university officials is whether universities are legally responsible for what their students do?

5. It reassures me that no one close to me has gotten into trouble.

6. It disturbs me that four university students will have to pay between $12,000 and $17,500 to the recording industry.

7. Many students are wondering if those students will be punished by university officials as well.

8. It's not clear why people continue to download without paying.

9. Something I'd like to know is if music companies are pursuing individual lawsuits abroad.

10. We have a right to know how much online privacy computer users have.